"Caution: Living May Be Hazardous"

"Caution:

Living May Be Hazardous"

Debunking the Happiness Myth

WALT MENNINGER, M.D.

SHEED ANDREWS AND McMEEL, INC.
Subsidiary of Universal Press Syndicate
KANSAS CITY

Library of Congress Cataloging in Publication Data

Menninger, Walt.
    "Caution, living may be hazardous".

    Based on the author's newsfeature column entitled
In-sights, distributed by the Universal Press Syndicate.
    1. Conduct of life— Addresses, essays, lectures
    I. Title.
BJ1581.2.M44   170'.202   78-23523
ISBN 0-8362-6501-7

For Connie
   the companion with whom I have
   the privilege of sharing life's
   pains and pleasures.

Contents

PART TWO

PART THREE

PART FOUR

Acknowledgments

For several years, it has been my privilege and responsibility to author a newsfeature column entitled In-Sights, distributed by the Universal Press Syndicate. In my writing, I have sought to help people gain greater insight into human behavior and to become more sensitive to psychological issues in human problems. The work of collecting material and organizing ideas for those columns has led to this book.

Obviously, a work of this nature draws upon the efforts of many people to whom I am most grateful. There are the many professional colleagues whose scientific reports I have sought to share in language which can be readily understood by the lay reader. There are the many readers of my columns who have responded with letters seeking more information or generously sharing their experiences. There are the many newspaper editors whose confidence in the In-Sights feature has sustained its presence as a Universal Press Syndicate offering.

I am appreciative of Jim Andrews and John McMeel, whose strong encouragement led to my assuming responsibility for writing the In-Sights feature; and especially am I grateful for the patient kibitzing and editorial support of Tom Drape, my editor with UPS, who helped develop the structure and organization of this book.

Finally, I must acknowledge the sources of inspiration for my writing—the examples set by my father, Dr. Will, and uncle, Dr.

Karl Menninger, in effectively articulating psychiatric concepts to increase public knowledge and understanding; and the stimulation to write prompted by a marvelous high school journalism teacher, Ruth Hunt.

—W. Walter Menninger, M.D.
August 1978
Topeka, Kansas

PART ONE

Caution

No doubt about it. There is a lot of pain in this world. Glance through most any daily newspaper, and you can't help but be reminded of the dangerous world in which we live. The following items appeared in one recent evening paper:

Oklahoma City (UPI)—Six restaurant employees, including four teenagers, were marched into a rear freezer room and methodically shot to death in the robbery of a restaurant along a busy interstate highway Sunday night.

Cairo, Egypt (AP)—A city bus packed with soldiers and workers swerved to miss a truck, smashed through a retaining wall and plunged into the Nile River, killing at least fifty-six passengers.

Golden, Colorado (UPI)—The National Earthquake Information Service says the world can expect at least one great earthquake, 18 major quakes and about 120 strong tremors—causing about ten thousand fatalities—in an average year.

Ottawa, Kansas (UPI)—A car attempting to pass a second vehicle at the crest of a hill east of the city was struck by a semitruck, killing five persons.

In the incidents reported from Oklahoma City, Cairo and Ottawa, people died suddenly and unexpectedly. Remaining behind are relatives and friends who must grapple painfully with the unanswerable questions—Why? What's to be done?

When we start out in life, we haven't the slightest idea of what we're getting into. The infant can't understand what the world is all about. But gradually, the developing baby does come to appreciate two important sensations—pleasure and pain. Pleasure is a desirable state of being; pain is undesirable. It doesn't take long for the child to appreciate the difference and to prefer the pleasurable states while protesting painful states. The infant thus becomes strongly motivated to operate on the basis of the pleasure principle, that is, to seek pleasure and avoid pain. That motivation persists all through life to influence much of human behavior.

The infant assumes that pleasure is good, because it is a pleasant feeling; and pain is bad, because it is an unpleasant feeling. Yet, is that always true? Can we be sure that pleasure is always good for us and pain is bad? Not necessarily. The decade of the 1970s has been marked by an increasing awareness that many things in life thought to be pleasurable and harmless were not so after all. First, there was the report of the USPHS Surgeon General's Advisory Panel on Smoking and Health, with its conclusion: cigarette smoking is hazardous to your health. Then medical researchers began to identify more and more substances which were not as innocuous as originally assumed: foods with a high cholesterol content; food additives like red dye No. 2, saccharin, cyclamates; the fire-retardant chemical Tris; the all-purpose insecticide DDT.

At the same time, uncomfortable though it may be, pain is not always such a bad thing. Pain is an important signal to the organism to alert it to some kind of injury or disorder. In its absence, one's survival may be threatened. The paraplegic who is without sensation in parts of his body is particularly vulnerable to injuries and infections which he cannot promptly sense and treat. One of the difficult aspects of cancer is that in its early stages it is a painless process. And controversy continues about the use of the pain-relieving drug butazolidine in race horses which overextend their abilities and damage their legs because of a resultant insensitivity to pain.

Further, much as we might prefer to avoid painful circumstances, they are inevitable in life. In order to survive, you have to develop some capacity to tolerate and cope with pain, both physical pain and psychological pain. Coping effectively with painful experiences can strengthen one and contribute to keeping life in a proper perspective.

Life is full of losses and hurts, most of which are not anticipated. People are often caught unawares by events like those reported in the newspaper—violent crimes, accidents, earthquakes—or such comparable incidents as a devastating tornado, a dam collapsing and flooding a peaceful valley, an airplane crash. Generally, these threats are perceived as all being external, beyond our control, the result of an act of God or some unknown stranger. That is not always true. In fact, a victim-offender survey in ten metropolitan cities completed for the National Commission on the Causes and Prevention of Violence found that only 16 percent of all murders are committed by strangers; 84 percent of homicides are committed by a relative, friend or acquaintance of the victim!

The popular fantasy that the dangers in life are all "out there" is also belied by the reports from the National Safety Council. Consistently, they find that more accidents occur in the home than anywhere else. Also, the vast majority of auto accidents occur within twenty-five miles of one's home. Of course, these findings are related to the fact that people spend the majority of their time in the home and the majority of their driving within twenty-five miles of their home.

The critical point is that there are hazards all around us which we must inevitably encounter if we are to live a normal life. The air we breathe has a host of foreign bodies in it, some natural and many added by the activities of man. The world teems with creatures, microscopic and macroscopic, all competing to survive. Unless you decide to retreat into a carefully filtered incubator, you are faced with frustrations of your wishes to achieve pleasure and avoid pain, and threats to your livelihood.

Life thus becomes a series of trade-offs, of calculated risks and probabilities. When you drive to the store to pick up some groceries, you realize at some level that between you and your destination are some obstructions—other drivers going their own way, roads torn up for utility repairs, etc. You usually figure the odds favor your making the journey safely, and the desire for the groceries justifies the risk. You don't anticipate colliding with some joy-riding adolescent who speeds through a stop sign, but that can and does happen.

Because you make the trip safely most of the time, you tend to minimize the risks. "Such things may happen to others, but not to me." You assume that you are invulnerable to such a happenstance. This assumption parallels the persistent denial of most people that life will sometime come to an end. Intellectually you may acknowledge that you won't live forever, but you just don't plan on dying—even though many people do hedge their bet by purchasing insurance.

When a painful event does occur—and one will, sooner or later—you react with hurt and resentment and bitterness. It shouldn't have happened. It's unfair, unjust! Somebody else must be responsible. Somebody is going to pay for this! (As if the pain and hurt you have experienced can really be assuaged by collecting some money or a pound of flesh.)

The adversity and pain in life are not always someone else's fault. Frequently, it is possible to identify the ways that people set themselves up to be hurt or injured. Sometimes the process may be conscious and deliberate; more often than not, it occurs subconsciously. Thus, careful studies of industrial accidents have found more than half of them result from some subconscious slip on the part of the person who is injured. The auto accident referred to in the newspaper item cited earlier occurred when the driver of the car tried to pass another car at the crest of a hill, in a no-passing zone.

In this context, I am reminded of some words by Dr. Karl Menninger in the opening chapter of *Man Against Himself*. After reviewing some of the "spectacular rages of Nature" against man, he makes this observation:

"One would expect that in the face of these overwhelming blows at the hands of Fate or Nature, man would oppose himself steadfastly to death and destruction in a universal brotherhood of beleaguered humanity. But this is not the case. Whoever studies the behavior of human beings cannot escape the conclusion that we must reckon with an enemy within the lines. It becomes increasingly evident that some of the destruction which curses the earth is self-destruction—the extraordinary propensity of the human being to join hands with external forces in an attack upon his own existence."

Pain and pleasure are both important motivating forces in life. We do much of what we do to diminish the former and increase the latter. The goals of eliminating pain and poverty and disease may be admirable, but they are unrealistic. Unless you can accept the fact that you will experience some grievous hurts in life, you are going to be even more devastated when they occur.

But how do you get people to face something they don't want to face? If you attempt to "tell it like it is," people tend to turn you off. They don't want to hear such things; they only want to hear what sounds pleasant and reassuring and fits with the world they prefer to believe exists.

What follows in this book are some brief essays which attempt to face up to some of the pains which are inevitable in life, and which may help keep some of life's experiences in perspective. This is not an encyclopedia of all life's painful situations, nor is it a guide to coping with all life's problems. Along the way, however, you find a sharing of experiences by others, and some thoughts which may make those painful moments in life more bearable.

A DEADLY FASCINATION

On Monday evening, December 29, 1975, eleven persons were killed outright and seventy-five others injured in a powerful bomb blast at New York's LaGuardia Airport. "A senseless act," said the President. But why? Why do people do such things? What is the sense?

Of course, we hear the misguided rationalizations used by terrorist bombers all over the world—SDS-Weathermen, IRA fanatics, Palestine Liberation Front guerrillas. They say it is to frighten and intimidate, to draw attention to their cause, and to give retribution for reputed wrongs done them.

But there's more to it than that. Their acts are an expression of rage, destructive aggression which has gone beyond civilized bounds and which prompts our sense of outrage.

We are appalled at the apparently unprincipled destruction of people and property. We think such acts must be the result of warped minds. Yet are the rest of us really so different? Certainly, a vast majority of people are fascinated by and enjoy explosions.

That is clearly obvious to me when I step outside at midnight on New Year's Eve. For at least thirty minutes or more, there is the constant bang-bang of firecracker blasts occurring all over town.

And on Sunday morning, November 23, 1975, ten thousand people gathered on the banks of the Kanawha River in Charleston, West Virginia, to watch an explosion demolish an old bridge. The *Charleston Daily Mail* attracted nationwide attention for the event and sponsored a "Blow Up the Bridge" contest to select the person to press the detonator.

The actual blast was viewed not only by the assembled multitude in Charleston, but by the nation, courtesy of the television networks. As described by the *Daily Mail*, "The blast set off by Mrs. (Barbara) Oros (contest winner) issued a thunderous boom and carved the bridge into sixty pieces, reducing the rusty hulk to a crumpled heap of steel girders protruding slightly from the water."

All this reminded me of my uncle's favorite essay, "Civilization and Its Discontents," by Sigmund Freud. In it, Freud observes, "The truth is that men are not gentle, friendly creatures wishing for love, who simply defend themselves if they are attacked. But a powerful measure of desire for aggression has to be reckoned as part of their instinctual environment."

Freud goes on: "The existence of this tendency to aggression which we can detect in ourselves and rightly presume to be present in others is the factor that disturbs our relations with our neighbors and makes it necessary for culture to institute its high standards. Civilized society is perpetually menaced with disintegration through this primary hostility of men towards one another."

Traditionally, aggression is a "masculine" trait. Women are supposed to be retiring and demure. But Mrs. Oros pressing the detonator in Charleston challenges that stereotype, as does the new female aggression evidenced in the presidential assassination attempts by Lynette Fromme and Sara Jane Moore.

The reality is that the aggressive emotional drive is present in all human beings. The challenge to society has been to channel that aggressive energy into constructive activity—to blowing up unneeded bridges rather than crowded airport lobbies.

It doesn't begin under control. One need only look at the destructive capacity of the two-year-old to be reminded of that. I've often said, not too facetiously, that we needn't have developed the atom bomb if we just turned the two-year-olds loose on the world. The "terrible twos" have temper tantrums that are magnificent explosions, limited only by their small size and muscular capacity.

In a frustrated rage, the two-year-old would like to destroy the world, and freely vents that rage insofar as he can. Though that open expression of rage must be brought under control as the child grows up, most people continue to experience a vicarious pleasure in the sudden, forceful release of aggressive energy which occurs in an explosion.

So it is that the fascination with explosions and destruction can be traced to some basic emotional forces in our personality. Out of control, the fascination can be deadly!

FREE TIME

"To do nothing at all is the most difficult thing in the world."—
Oscar Wilde.

"God, how I hate Sundays. I am driven to all sorts of activities. I can't call a day my own . . . When there is nothing there
that I am supposed to do, then it gets unbearable." In these
words, a thirty-five-year-old successful artist described his reaction to free time.

A thirty-year-old woman writer put it this way: "I am depressed over weekends. I'm upset because time is my own. I have
free days, but I can't utilize them. I'm tense. I have a drink to feel
less tense . . . In my time off at night, I spend hours shopping in
stores."

How often have you looked forward to a holiday, only to find
that when it arrived, you couldn't make use of it? How many
people do you know who can't take a vacation without working?
They just can't relax.

Some people, for all their talk about enjoying a day off, work
just as furiously on that day as on any regular work day—but at
jobs in the yard or around the house. Such people have been
labeled workaholics, because of their inability to relax.

For more and more people, this is a problem. As a result of
shorter working days and weeks, longer vacations and labor-
saving devices, American people have more free time at their

disposal today than ever before.

Psychoanalyst Alexander Martin believes that this increase in free time confronts us with an adaptational crisis, because our culture does not prepare people to relax and make the most creative use of free time.

Instead, our culture reflects its heritage in the puritan work ethic. Relaxation is suppressed, discouraged and scorned. It is equated with idleness, sloth, apathy and laziness. Historical references to this view are easy to find.

Witness the old English proverb: "An idle brain is the devil's workshop." Or the words of the seventeenth century writer, Jeremy Collier: "Idleness is an inlet to disorder and makes way for licentiousness. People who have nothing to do are quickly tired of their own company."

Such exhortations imply that within man are evil impulses which will surface if he is not kept constantly occupied.

That view seemed to be confirmed in cases studied by Sandor Ferenczi, who wrote a paper on "Sunday Neuroses" over fifty years ago. He treated persons who had depression on their one free day a week.

He discovered that occurring within one typical person was a sense of "impulses much too dangerous for him to control which he must guard against." Therefore, he could not relax. he could not trust himself as his own master and instead had to rely on some external authority.

Martin, in his work, found a number of symptoms or behaviors which reflect an emotional inability to handle free time. Besides depression, he noted psychosomatic symptoms, compulsive behavior and a "spoil-sport" attitude which is relieved only when the individual makes himself a "slave" to external demands—work, family, an organization, etc.

13

Such people are unable to relax, even when the leisure time may be "earned." A tyrannical conscience prevents their enjoying free time as a rewarding, enlightening and self-fulfilling adventure.

Martin believes present-day education is directed toward making us "functional," and it doesn't prepare us for life off the job. Education for life off the job should be directed toward making people more resourceful and more able to be relaxed in body, mind and spirit.

"WE HAVEN'T GOT ANY POWER"

It was a little after ten P.M. when our friends called. "How would you like to come over and have a glass of wine by candlelight? A bolt of lightning struck an electric transformer on our block and we haven't got any power."

This was the same day that over fifteen thousand square miles of southern Florida and almost three million people were left without electricity. That power outage was attributed to the short circuit of a faulty fifty dollar relay switch, and some localities were without electricity for as long as seven hours.

These events inevitably bring to mind the massive power failure in the northeastern U.S. and neighboring Canada in November, 1965. But I was also reminded of a personal experience eleven years ago. At that time, a tornado marched within four blocks of our house and took power lines along with it.

Our reaction to the loss of electric power following the tornado went through several phases. The first evening, the family was still somewhat shocked at our narrow escape. Homes were demolished just a few blocks away.

When it got dark, we got our candles and flashlights. But it wasn't too easy to read by candlelight. Except for the transistor radio, there wasn't much to distract us. The television and stereo were silent. So we all went to bed early.

The next morning, we were forced to change some of our

regular routines. There was no electric clock-radio to wake us up. No electricity for the razor. Flick the electric toothbrush switch and nothing happened. The toaster-oven was useless; likewise the kitchen range.

We transferred food from our freezer to a neighbor's who still had power. But we washed our dishes in our sink, not the dishwasher. No housecleaning with the vacuum cleaner. No use of the clothes washer and dryer. Listen for the knock at the front door; the electric doorchimes weren't working.

And so it went. That evening we ate out. Back home, it was still a bit of an adventure with the candles; but we again went to bed with the sunset.

By the second morning, we were feeling somewhat edgy without electricity. But since so many people had suffered more serious inconvenience and losses, we could hardly complain. We just hoped the power company would get us back into operation as soon as possible.

Preparing for bed that evening, the adventure was definitely gone. Now, the candles were getting "old." Again, we hit the pad early. Some time later, I was awakened by a buzzing sound. And I realized that a light was on in the hallway.

Eureka! After fifty-four hours, the power was back on! The buzz? That was the electric toothbrush, finally responding to having been turned on the first morning after.

In retrospect, we didn't suffer too much. We weren't trapped in an elevator, or a subway (like some eight hundred thousand people in New York City in 1965). We weren't frustrated by nonfunctioning gas station pumps, or bank deposit calculators, or beauty shop machines, as in the recent Florida experience.

Can you imagine the consternation in the newsroom of a totally computerized modern newspaper when a power failure makes inaccessible or wipes out of the computer all the accumulated stories for one edition?

As we sipped some wine with our friends, in response to their invitation, we were reminded of how much we take electricity for granted—until we haven't got it. Then we realize how dependent we are on this energy; much more so than petroleum.

It may be a fun experience for a few hours, a holiday, an adventure. But it's kind of frightening, and humbling too. Despite all our giant technological achievements a bolt of lightning, a tornado, or a faulty relay switch can cut us down to size and make us pretty helpless.

WHY DO WE HAVE TO PAY TAXES?

As the income tax service commercials on television increase in frequency, we are reminded that the April 15 deadline is just around the corner.

Along with that deadline comes a renewal of the feelings provoked by those taxes and the energy and effort they represent. For the most part, people experience taxes as a loss of earnings, the government taking away money which is rightfully yours.

At a party several years ago, I overheard several people bragging about how much they were getting away with in taxes. They figured out how to take advantage of all the loopholes, and they took great pride in paying as little tax money as possible to the government.

That conversation bugged me then, and it stills does today! Those people were enjoying all the fruits of our democratic society, and all they could think of was how to minimize their responsibility for paying a share of the costs of government.

There are few places in this world with all the freedom, mobility and opportunity we have in this country. We can travel thousands of miles without crossing a guarded border or being searched by customs, without having to speak a foreign language or use a different currency. We can speak out and challenge ideas, policies and laws which we believe are wrong and in need of change.

We can take advantage of an incredible range of governmental services. There are state colleges and universities; federal and state hospitals or medicare and medicaid insurance. Governmental agencies enforce the law, inspect food products, review medications and drugs, search for causes of disease and control epidemics, etc.

If you add up all these services which the government provides, and then add to them all the special benefits of living in our free society, you must conclude that we've got a pretty good deal!

Beyond this realization, I would like to suggest viewing taxes from another perspective. When I was in junior high school, I remember being much impressed by the fact that only 4 to 6 percent of all the energy generated by a steam locomotive ends up being applied to the rails to move the train. The remaining 94 to 96 percent of energy is lost in heat and friction.

Granted, the steam engine is not a model of efficiency. We think we should be able to do much better in our own lives. Yet we tend to assume that we should be 100 percent efficient in every way. In return for our effort in life, we should get 100 percent personal benefit.

But that's impossible! Realistically, we have to anticipate something less, some "losses." Our take-home pay or net income is not going to be 100 percent of our gross income. A certain percentage is going to be spent in assuring an orderly society in which we can work—and that percentage is collected in the form of taxes.

There are other inevitable losses. Some are predictable and regular. Others are not, like accidents or a natural disaster, events which have their costs in energy and income. While we may be particularly sensitive to the lost part of energy and income, we should be grateful that our "efficiency" is as good as it is, and so much better than, for instance, that of the steam engine.

Of course, people will always have some feelings of envy and resentment about the fact that everyone does not pay exactly the same in life. And we can expect an eternal search for some formula which will equalize the burden.

Every new effort at "tax reform" is a fresh attempt to adjust the obligations and determine a "fair share" or a "fair loss" for each taxpayer.

I don't have much hope that the latest proposals will really come any closer to being a magical solution to the inequities of taxes. The various special interest groups will take their toll. Nevertheless, I do believe that if you add up what we get for our tax dollar, no matter how inefficient you may think government is, it's still a fantastic bargain—and cheap at many times the price!

ARE YOU AN OPTIMIST OR A PESSIMIST?

You sit down at the counter and the waitress gives you a twelve ounce glass containing only six ounces of water. How do you react? How do you describe it?

Is it half-full? If you think of it that way, you are a positive thinker. As such, you will enjoy the words and sayings of other positive thinkers. One of those to whom you might respond is Ella Wheeler Wilcox, a famous American poet who lived from 1855 to 1919.

Her orientation is reflected in "Whatever Is, Is Best," which is both the title of one of her poems and the title of a collection of her published poems:

> I know, as my life grows older,
>   And mine eyes have clearer sight—
> That under each rank Wrong, somewhere,
>   There lies the root of Right.
> That each sorrow has its purpose—
>   By the sorrowing oft unguessed,
> But as sure as the Sun brings morning,
>   Whatever is, is best.
>
> I know that each sinful action,
>   As sure as the night brings shade,

Is sometime, somewhere, punished,
　　Though the hour may be long delayed.
I know that the soul is aided
　　Sometimes by the heart's unrest,
And to grow, means often to suffer—
　　But whatever is, is best.

I know there are no errors,
　　In the great Eternal plan,
And all things work together
　　For the final good of man.
And I know when my soul speeds onward
　　In the grand, Eternal quest,
I shall say, as I look back earthward,
　　Whatever is, is best.

But what about the opposite? It's not half-full, but half-empty!
Such a perspective identifies you as one who is keenly aware of
being deprived. And your resonance is with Murphy's Law:
"Whatever can possibly go wrong, will."

Devotees of Murphy have been blessed of late by two compil-
ations of his law and its various corollaries: *Russell on "Murphy's Law,"* by Jim Russell (Celestial Arts), and *Murphy's Law
and Other Reasons Why Things Go ¡ƃuoɹM* by Arthur Block
(Price/Stern/Sloan).

Russell offers a discussion of variations of "Anything that can
go wrong, will go wrong." Things will go wrong at the worst
possible time. If there is a possibility of several things going
wrong, the one that will go wrong is the one that will do the most
damage. Left to themselves, things will go from bad to worse.
Nature always sides with the hidden flaw. If everything seems to

be going well, you have obviously overlooked something.

He goes on to apply the law in a wide range of situations: Interchangeable parts won't; leakproof seals will; any wire, pipe, board cut to exact length will be 5/8-inch too short; a three hundred dollar color TV picture tube will protect a ten cent fuse by blowing first, etc.

Bloch's collection traces the law back to Captain Ed Murphy, a development engineer with the Wright Field Aircraft Lab in the late 1940s. Bloch goes beyond Murphy, including "the wit and wisdom of our most delightfully demented technologists, bureaucrats, humanists and antisocial observers."

He cites laws from Murphy and Parkinson to Peter's Principle and Tritschmann's Paradox ("A pipe gives a wise man time to think and a fool something to stick in his mouth"). He gives one commentary on Murphy's Law which I first heard from the former chairman of the board of Bristol-Myers, Frederic Schwartz: "Murphy was an optimist!"

IF YOU WANT TO QUIT SMOKING . . .

A colleague was celebrating his fifty-first birthday. As he lit up his cigarette and took a deep drag, he leaned back and said, "This is it. I'm giving up cigarettes after today."

A hundred-thousand doctors have given up smoking. My colleague has tried before, but he hasn't yet succeeded in kicking the habit. Few confirmed smokers find it an easy thing to do, for smoking meets some definite psychological (and sometimes physical) needs.

Why is it not easy? Any change in habits is discomfiting. The only reason you sustain a change in your behavior is because the pluses add up to more than the minuses—what you gain is better than what you've now got.

And what you gain from smoking is not always immediately apparent, while the losses most surely are.

Studies make it clear that one gain of not smoking is a greater life expectancy and less likelihood of lung cancer, heart disease and emphysema (a lung condition that reduces the oxygen-carbon dioxide change in the lungs).

These studies demonstrate further that there is a direct correlation between the years of smoking and increased chances of disease. Thus, any time you stop, your health odds are better.

There are other gains more immediately apparent. With the reduction of irritation to nasal and bronchial passages, the sense of smell improves, the hacking cough fades.

Food will taste better, along with the improved smell. Your cigarette breath will no longer be so obvious—to yourself or those around you. You will no longer burn cigarette holes in your clothing, or the furniture, or rugs, or tablecloths.

What do you lose when you give up smoking? A habit which may give you a special sense of relaxation or tension relief, especially during periods when you are under pressure. An activity which offers a change of pace and something to do with your hands.

You will also lose an activity which in some prevents weight gain. Indeed, one of the less desirable "gains" of stopping for some people is a weight gain, the result of a tendency to eat more and thereby compensate for the loss of smoking pleasure.

Are fewer health hazards and better-tasting food worth the present loss of smoking pleasure? Only you can decide those values for yourself. And if you intend to give up smoking, rest assured it will take a good bit of will power, a strong motivation based on the conviction it really is best for you. As one health educator put it, "Nothing succeeds like will power and a little blood in the sputum."

How do you go about it? There is no one sure way. Different people may find different approaches successful. Some decide to quit impulsively; others plan carefully ahead for the quitting day.

Some emphasize their will power; some keep a score card; some take advantage of group support—family members, others going through the same experience. Some go cold turkey; others gradually cut down.

If you're seriously interested in kicking the smoking habit, there are a number of places you can turn. One is the local chapter of the American Cancer Society. They should have available a delightful and straightforward pamphlet, *If You Want To Give Up Cigarettes*.

The pamphlet offers a number of concrete suggestions, as well as answers to questions. Some thoughts on "Quitting Day": Drink frequent glasses of water; nibble fruit, celery, carrots, etc. Be vigorous, exercise. Use your lungs—deep breaths of fresh air can be wonderfully calming. Reward yourself.

What if you fail to make it? As the Cancer Society pamphlet observes, "Don't be discouraged. Many thousands who finally stopped did so only after several attempts."

LIVING CAN BE DANGEROUS
FOR YOUR HEALTH

Dear Dr. Menninger:

I am past menopause and have been taking a tablet containing estrogen off and on now for six or seven years. I am very worried about estrogen, and as yet I haven't gotten a satisfactory answer from my doctor.

I have been troubled with hot flashes for ten years, and this estrogen preparation is the only thing my doctor has prescribed for me. He also tells me it is better for my bones and general health. And I do feel better.

Yet, after reading some articles and hearing comments on television, I constantly worry if it is safe to take. And I have stopped taking it.

Will you please comment on this problem?

Respectfully,
Mrs. F. P.

For many years, estrogen preparations have been used to relieve symptoms associated with menopause. And the hormone has been helpful in keeping bones from losing calcium.

But recently, there has been an increasing awareness that some complications occur more often in women taking estrogen than those who don't—an increased incidence of a cancer of the uterus, of gall bladder disease and of abnormal blood clotting.

27

Because of these increased complications, the Food and Drug Administration has directed suppliers of estrogen preparations to alert persons taking the substance. Effective October 18, 1977, all persons receiving estrogen preparations were also to receive information about its risks.

How much is the risk? Cancer of the uterus accounts for roughly 7 percent of the 343,000 new cancer cases reported in women annually in this country. The risk of a woman taking estrogen of having cancer of the lining of the uterus (endometrial cancer) is about five to ten times greater than for a woman not taking estrogen.

Further, the endometrial cancer risk is greater the longer you take estrogen or the higher the dose of estrogen you take. Thus, if you do take the medication, it is best to take the lowest possible dose for the shortest possible time.

The action by the FDA to inform estrogen users of the risks is part of that agency's responsibility to protect the population from adverse effects of food and drugs.

It seems, however, that almost every time you turn around, another substance is being implicated as hazardous to your health. Most people are quite familiar with the health risks of cigarette-smoking.

Because of a presumptive cancer-causing potential, red dye No. 2 and cyclamates were withdrawn from the market. Recent findings have put the spotlight on saccharin, a nitrite substance used to preserve bacon and a hair-coloring chemical.

All this information does leave one in a dilemma. How do you balance, in the case of estrogen, the remote possibility of a complication like cancer or gall bladder disease or thrombophlebitis, with the immediate relief of disturbing hot flashes.

There is no easy answer. Hopefully, as you consider your

decision, you have as many facts as possible at your disposal.

Yet, the dilemma should be kept in a broad perspective. All life involves risks and trade-offs. There is no guarantee that any substance you eat or use is totally free of some potential complication.

Everyone should be reminded as they arise each day: "Caution—Living can be dangerous for your health!"

A TOWN IN THE GRIP OF HYSTERIA

Few events may arouse the level of fear and anxiety in a community as a senseless murder. This was demonstrated again in a small midwestern community where a state institution for mentally retarded persons is located.

One of the institution residents walked away from his assignment and a few blocks from the institution senselessly killed a little girl who was on her way to kindergarten.

You can imagine the outcry in the town. The news dominated the local scene. The governor of the state was prompted to issue a statement. The townsfolk drew up a petition demanding the institution be surrounded by a fence, and that none of the institution residents attend the local schools.

A young high school editor attended the hearing on the petition, and then penned her perspective in the high school paper. Her courageous editorial is worth sharing:

"Welcome to [our town], America, at its finest; complete with resident bigots, feet-kissing city officials and by far the most narrow, conservative, 'Let's get the damned weirdo-freaks out of here' attitude possible! Oh yes, right here we have the pride of [our section of the state].

"Recently, I attended the special city commission meeting concerning the death of [the little girl] and the [institution for the mentally retarded]. Until that evening, I could almost like our town, but now this town could fall into the nearest ocean and I wouldn't bat an eyelash.

"You see, there are many people who seem to think that the training center is a jail and its patients are prisoners. Speakers at the meeting kept saying 'the inmates' and 'escapees.' People seem to forget that the residents of the center are not jailed convicts, nor are they animals to be locked away. Many people seem to feel that the sole purpose of the center is to keep 'those retarded freaks' locked away from the rest of us 'good ole plain and simple, God fearin' Americans.'

"Well, wake up. this town is on the skids and dying fast, not because there is no industry, but because no one really cares about the rest of the world. The center is an internationally known, widely-respected institution which for more than twenty-five years has been a leader in the education and care of the mentally retarded. In twenty-five years, and after several thousand patients, this center has had no serious incidents involving a resident of this town.

"The center has a better record than our senior high school—remember the fights last year and the police cars constantly dragging the island, waiting for a riot to break out?

"The center has provided jobs for both adults and teenagers in this community and has put an untold amount of money into its economy. Yet members of this community are up in arms against an institution that has benefited so many thousands of people.

"If you look closely at the petition, you notice that it not only is rather illogical but is also illegal and unfair . . . The petition is a product of fear. Hysteria has gripped the town and everyone is hiding behind a petition using fear as a substitute for reason.

"As long as residents of this town let fear, anger and bigotry govern their actions, then this town will continue to lose its fight

31

for survival and will end up as an empty shell, left to remind the world of what it and the center could have been."

IN A DEMOCRACY, THE MAJORITY
IS ALWAYS WRONG

In high school, I had a cynical physics teacher who insisted that "in a democracy, the majority is always wrong." In recent years, I have had more than one occasion to wonder about the truth of his statement.

We may be of a species known as homo sapiens—wise man—but when you observe our political behavior, you can't help but wonder just how wise we are, and whom can you trust.

Californians have been warned for years to anticipate earthquakes, which they assume are beyond their control. The major upheaval in California (June 1978) wasn't the result of any subterranean shift, yet it sent shock waves throughout the country.

It was the disruption in local governments forced by the passage of Proposition 13, the property tax limit. The news media followed the aftershocks of this "tax revolt" in community after community—summer-school closings, municipal personnel layoffs, a state hiring freeze, etc.

At the same time, it's become evident that many people either didn't fully appreciate the impact of the passage of that referendum or didn't really believe that a reduction in tax revenue would necessarily force a reduction in tax-funded programs.

Yet, it's not hard to understand why some people did vote for the tax rollback, having just received property tax assessments that suggested doubling and tripling of their tax bills. When that happens to you, it's hard to be dispassionate and logical about the police budget.

One of the limitations of most legislators is that they feel they must pass some laws or they won't be doing their job. Wouldn't it be wonderful to have a legislative session where instead of the compulsion to add more laws to the statute books, there was a commitment to remove some?

Regrettably, as in the case of the California proposition, many laws get passed without there being any real appreciation of the impact of the new law.

In this day and age of trying to protect the world from unanticipated damage, which results from impulsive and thoughtless activities of homo sapiens, maybe we should require an "environmental impact" statement before consideration can proceed on any law.

That seems like a great idea, except we'd probably have no reliable prediction we could depend on. The *Wall Street Journal* recently reviewed some environmental impact statements prepared a few years ago for some major building projects, and the accuracy of the predictions was really quite poor.

Further, any issue which touches emotions will find people with their minds made up; in those cases, people simply disregard statements that don't agree with their preconceived notions. That seems to happen in discussions about the Equal Rights Amendment.

A survey of the impact of certain laws—drug control laws—was recently prepared by Dr. George R. Edison, who works with the student health service at the University of Utah.

In the *Journal of the American Medical Association,* Edison looked at the treatment effects of drug laws and concluded that "as treatment, drug laws appear to be only marginally effective. Their side effects are so dangerous that the treatment is often more devastating than the disease."

He reviews the underlying reasons for the laws, the overt purposes of them, their effectiveness, and the dangers of the laws both to society and to individuals.

He acknowledges that the intention of the drug laws is not so much to prevent damage as to express a moral judgment. But he observes that "a judgment based strictly on the effectiveness and safety of drug laws would require their immediate repeal or overhaul."

GUN OWNERS—PARANOID, FRIGHTENED, INSECURE CITIZENS?

America is the most powerful, prosperous, technically capable, secure nation in the world. But it seems to be populated by an incredible number of paranoid, frightened, insecure citizens.

What else can you conclude after the fantastic outpouring of mail to the Treasury Department's Bureau of Alcohol, Tobacco and Firearms protesting a proposed regulation to require gun manufacturers to stamp special serial numbers on each firearm they make?

So many letters were written about that proposal that the department had to extend the deadline for comments. It's quite clear that the vast majority of writers (fifteen-to-one) have great fears about any potential gun regulations.

Of course, it shouldn't be surprising that so many letters came forth—that's consistent with reactions to any proposal regarding guns. And it's another illustration of the domination of reason by emotion, with a response similar to that when one touches an exposed nerve.

Actually, the proposed regulation does not restrict gun ownership. It is designed to make it easier to trace illegally used firearms. As such, the regulation has the support of the International Association of Chiefs of Police and the Police Foundation.

However, the regulation is perceived by highly emotional and militant gun owners and the National Rifle Association as an encroachment upon free and unrestricted access to weapons.

Their reaction reflects an attitude similar to what I label the "Little Dutch Boy and the Dike" phenomenon. That is, they assume that any small breach in the area of gun identification is like a trickle of water breaching the dike. It is assumed further that the trickle will inevitably erode the dike to become a rivulet, then a stream, then a river, and finally a flood.

The "flood" for gun owners is the end of all protection of the right for each citizen to bear arms. Thus, any regulation which might lead to possible identification and tracing of guns is seen as the first step toward ultimate confiscation of all weapons from law-abiding, decent citizens.

Honestly! They have no faith that there might be some reasonable and dependable alternative between the extremes of unfettered, untraceable gun ownership and total confiscation.

In that sense, they are fixed with the all-or-nothing perception of the world that characterizes the child. The child finds it very difficult to understand that there might be a middle ground. Rather, he simplifies the world by putting everything into either/or terms. Either it's this way or that. Either you're for me or against me. There's no in-between.

The proposed regulation comes at an interesting time—on the tenth anniversary of the assassination of Senator Robert F. Kennedy, which prompted President Johnson to appoint the National Commission on the Causes and Prevention of Violence. Under the chairmanship of Dr. Milton Eisenhower, I had the privilege of serving on that commission.

One of the hot issues we addressed was the relationship of guns and crime and violence. And there is a relationship, whether people like to face it or not. However, the problem is not with all guns, but simply with one class—the handgun, which is the common instrument of violent crime and assassination.

If one believes that violent crime should be reduced, one significant step has to be establishing some limits on the access of potential criminals to the weapon most commonly used—the handgun.

However, it's exceedingly difficult to carry on a rational discussion of potential limits or controls on the access to such guns, because so many people react as if their personal security is threatened by such a prospect. For these people, their minds are made up.

One may only speculate about what really is behind the intensity of these people's feelings—a sense of insecurity, a need to have access to a gun in order to sustain a sense of adequacy and potency in a fearful world.

IF WE MAKE MISTAKES,
WE JUST HAVE TO LIVE WITH THEM

When you realize that you've made a mistake in life, the natural tendency is to try to undo it, to make up for it. That was the thrust of Linda Shipley's letter. At age sixteen, she gave up a child for adoption; and now, twelve years later, she regrets her decision.

Her letter sparked a number of responses, including some from adopted children, now grown, describing their search for biological roots. Here are some additional thoughts on the adoption issue—from the perspective of the adopting parent.

Dear Dr. Menninger:

I read Mrs. Shipley's letter with interest. I have two natural, and four adopted children. I have also lost three children by miscarriages, one of whom lived thirty minutes. So I feel I can empathize with almost anyone.

Mrs. Shipley had the option at age sixteen of placing her child in foster homes until she was able to assume full care of her. At this point, she is looking back at her sixteen-year-old self with the maturity of her twenty-eight years, and deciding she should not have put the child up for adoption.

But we must all live and make decisions when events occur in our lives. We don't get to do it in retrospect. If we make mistakes, we just have to live with them. That's life.

Suppose at age twenty-eight, after being married for ten years, I had said, "I really made a mistake when I had this child, and I really don't want to rear her." Society (and I suspect Mrs. Shipley, too) would say, "You have to live with your mistake."

Biology says you are technically a mother when you give birth, but that is only the tip of the iceberg. I am grateful to the biological mothers of my adopted children, but these children are mine.

I am the one who has cared for them, nurtured them, educated them, disciplined them. And I see no reason for them ever to be confronted by their biological mother whose interest at such a late date is only self-serving and maudlin.

Sincerely,
Mrs. E. M.

Dear Dr. Menninger:

Mrs. M. M. of California wrote about her search for her natural parent and the happy ending. Let me give you an insight on the other side, the side of the adoptive parent.

We have two natural-born daughters and two adopted sons. We took both boys to be our very own, one when he was two days old, the other as a foster son when he was sixteen. He asked us to adopt him, and we did.

Within a year, he wanted us to help him find his natural mother. Because we thought we understood the agony he was going through, we wanted his life to be complete, we agreed to help him.

As Mrs. M. M. said, I remember the phone call all too well. He talked to his mother. They were so happy and arranged to meet. She told him everything he knew about her was a lie. (Thank God it was not information we had given him.)

Did we really make the mistake? We wanted your child; you didn't. Now that you've changed your mind, we stand convicted. We loved your son as much as we possibly could; now we are the scapegoats for your mistake. There is no room in his life for us.

We were good babysitters while you lived your life and needed a place for your child to grow up. We spoiled him. We overlooked his bad points, because of the rough breaks he had. We encouraged him to make his life worthwhile. We wanted him to be forgiving of you, because no one can live with hate.

Well, it ended as Mrs. M. M. said, with a "happy ending." But a happy ending for whom? We still have his picture, a pair of faded old jeans, part of a chess set he loved, and many memories.

Have you ever tried to console parents when they have lost a child? There are no words!

Mrs. S. W.

TELL IT LIKE IT IS

Tell it like it is! That's a popular observation. Yet, all too often when you do tell it like it is, you discover that people get upset. They don't really want to hear it like it is; they want to hear it like they want it to be.

I've found this to be true not only with public issues, like gun control or school busing, but also with personal concerns. Most of us don't like to hear bad things about ourselves. We resist facing up to such things, turning them off or tuning them out when they don't fit with what we want.

Generally, when we are presented with something that doesn't fit our view of the world or ourselves, we get angry. This is reflected in the oft-noted phenomenon of rejecting the bearer of bad news, like the ancient Greeks punished the messenger who brought bad tidings.

Anytime that one stands up to be counted and to say something that touches on an emotionally charged issue, one is sure to provoke a reaction. When what is said is not what people want to hear, the reaction can be quite intense. All through history, there are examples of the price people have paid when they followed the dictates of their conscience or intellect to tell it as they saw it.

Galileo was one such individual. Early in his life, he determined that Copernicus was right in saying that the Earth was just a planet and not the center of the universe. However, it wasn't until the discovery of the telescope that Galileo confirmed the theory through direct observations.

In 1610, the Catholic church and its official scientists had other ideas. The Earth was the center of the universe and everything revolved around us. That was the cornerstone of their theories. As they had earlier rejected Copernicus's contentions, they were most upset with Galileo.

Galileo's insistence on telling it like it is resulted in his house arrest for many years and his conviction of "crimes" by the church. The authorities were particularly provoked because Galileo not only expressed his views publicly, he did so in the language of the people, Italian, instead of the language of the church and science, Latin.

What does it mean that one speaks in the language of the people? How much does that threaten the established order? Quite a bit in the case of Galileo. There remains even today some suspicion about any scientist who doesn't abide by the traditional manner to communicate his findings and views.

In my medical school days, I recall snide comments about those members of the profession who reported their findings in *Time*, or *Newsweek* or the *New York Times*, rather than in the traditional professional journals.

How safely can we express our views, when they are an exception or contrary to the prevailing view? Will people tolerate a challenge when "like it is" isn't like they want it to be? As John Locke commented in "An Essay on Human Understanding," also written in the seventeenth century: "New opinions are always suspected, and usually opposed, without any other reason but because they are not already common."

I'm committed to telling it like it is. I've found it a special challenge to help people face some painful realities. Repeatedly, my patients have shared with me a reluctance to admit some things about themselves. Sometimes it is because they feel if I knew the awful truth, I'd have nothing to do with them.

All of us have a struggle with unacceptable feelings in ourselves which we don't want to face—our hates or fears or forbidden desires. Most often we put the lid on these thoughts and feelings, "filing" them in the recesses of our mind, concerned that any expression of these ideas will destroy our world. Hopefully, we can learn to face such things openly and cope with them without being destroyed.

We all have a personal responsibility to do a better job of telling ourselves "like it is" in our own lives. At the same time, we have to confront society with its hypocrisies and challenge people to be fully responsible for their inconsistencies. We must constantly seek to hear it like it is and control our urge to strike out irrationally when like it is isn't what we want it to be.

PART TWO

Living

Life often seems to progress automatically, like a flowing river, with some stretches of turbulent rapids and others more placid and meandering. Both seen and unseen forces direct the course of the river from its origins to its termination in the sea. The course of life—the pattern of living—is likewise determined by both seen and unseen forces.

Homo sapiens—"wise man"—has become the dominant species on earth because of two remarkable features—the opposable thumb which allows the hand to grasp and be used as a tool as few other species can do; and an elaborate forebrain, which with more than 10^{13} neuronal connections is truly the most remarkable computer ever created. The development of the brain has permitted mankind and womankind to learn not only from experience, but to develop an elaborate capacity to share and transmit that experience through language, both spoken and printed. Knowledge is thus stored and passed across boundaries of space and time, increasing our ability not only to survive but to enjoy the fruits of the accumulated knowledge and skills of our ancestors.

These unique capacities of homo sapiens have been used in pursuit of the pleasure principle—to make life easier and more comfortable. Much of modern technology has been devoted to just this purpose, with appliances that diminish the time and energy required to prepare meals, wash clothes, clean the house, look after the yard. It has likewise allowed us to control our climate with air conditioning and heating and have instant entertainment and reassuring companionship through radio, television and telephones.

The pleasure principle is but one of the unseen forces which profoundly influence the pattern of living. A number of other important forces also play a role in human behavior and affect the adaptive capacity of individuals. Foremost among those forces are feelings. It may be reassuring to realize that the rational, thinking ability of men and women through the ages has led to a fantastic accumulation of knowledge and to the development of our civilization and modern technology. But all through history, one finds the powerful influence of emotions on the course of events. All too often, one sees behavior that is less motivated by careful, rational, civilized thought than by emotional pressures of affection, desire, lust, envy, resentment, or rage. Upon careful examination, these powerful emotional forces may be identified as some variation of the two great emotional experiences people have in life—love and hate. The expression of these feelings by children is generally tolerated and sometimes even cute, but as children grow into maturity, restraints are invoked. Open expression by adults of either love or hate, except in carefully protected situations, is not well tolerated. It's all right to make love in your own bedroom, but not on the Capitol steps. It's all right to fight as long as you wear gloves, break after three minute intervals and have a referee to make sure nobody hits below the belt; but it's not all right on the street, with weapons.

Another significant influence on the pattern of living is the impact of early life experience, which "programs" our computer-like brain. In contrast to the programming of the usual computer, certain aspects of life serve to complicate that programming and introduce distortions. For instance, the sensory input which programs the brain comes not only from the outside—how we're treated by our parents and other people—but from internal body sensations and desires. Further, this programming starts while the brain is still immature. At birth and during childhood the nerve fibers are not all fully functional and the brain only achieves full maturity during adolescent years. Thus, the infant's thinking pattern limits the understanding of life events, a thinking pattern which is marked by seeing the world in concrete and self-referent terms. Whatever happens is presumed to happen because of something the child did or didn't do. Abstract concepts—the complexity of the world; what is death, religion, occupation; why are there sexual differences—are beyond the child's comprehension. Rather, he searches for simple explanations in black and white terms, and acts accordingly.

Consider, for instance, the impossible dilemma for the developing child to understand why and how what he takes in—"eat your spinach and drink your milk, they're good for you"—is so good and necessary, and yet what comes out, his bowel movement and urine, is so bad. Why? There must be something basically bad inside oneself if good things taken in turn into bad things. An adult may view such a dilemma as silly; but throughout life, people continue to struggle with "goodness" and "badness" within.

Yet another complication of the "programming" process of the youngster is the fact that his physical size makes it impossible for him to put in "adult" perspective all the sensations and events he experiences. The initial learning occurs while living in the land of giants, when everything seems so much larger and more overwhelming and when you are so insignificant and helpless. Then, not only does the individual change from infant to child to adolescent to adult, but the world is also constantly changing. During growth and development, you must modify and change your understanding both of yourself and the world in which you live. Inevitably, distortions of what life is really all about get programmed into your brain, and most computer experts acknowledge that once you program an error into a computer, it's well nigh impossible to get it out. So it is with all of us. And those errors continue to influence how we think about and relate to others, often without our having any conscious awareness of its happening. Our choice of the people with whom we like to associate, our patterns for relating to people in authority— bosses, police—will consistently reflect our early life experiences with the significant people in our life. Our likes and dislikes will generally parallel their likes and dislikes. And if some childhood experiences left us with unresolved conflicts, we will continue to seek solutions to those conflicts in adult life. If a child grows up loved and wanted and treated as if he is of value and worth, his adult attitude toward himself and others will reflect that. If a child is abused, taken advantage of and treated as an unwanted bother, his adult self-concept will likewise reflect that origin; and he is likely to pass those attitudes on to others with whom he comes in contact.

Once set, this patterning operates automatically, beyond our conscious awareness. Fixed in the subconscious depths of our personality, it ever after influences our behavior. Because it operates unconsciously, most people do not realize the degree to which their "deliberate" and "rational" decisions are actually heavily biased by those early experiences.

Children have great difficulty understanding and accepting differences. If one child has the latest toy, his best friend feels he should have one too. The operating premise is that "everybody should be like me." Faced with a difference, the child assumes that either something is wrong in the world or with "me." To reconcile the difference, he may deny that there really is a difference or else develop an elaborate explanation to achieve the same purpose. This is demonstrated in the responses of young children to questions about differences between boys and girls. They search for a simple explanation because the complex, abstract truth is beyond them. They tend to look at things in either/or, all-or-nothing terms. Either you are like me and for me, or you are unlike me and against me. Similarly, it's hard for the child to accept both good and bad existing in the same person or the fact that one can have opposing feelings toward the same object. Yet, it's quite clear that sometimes Mommy is loving, giving and wonderful; and other times she is angry, hurtful, and takes away things which the child wants. How can you love someone and also hate them at the same time? That's a mind-boggler, not only for the child but, since childhood patterns of thinking get carried over, also for adults. The tendency persists in most adults to search for the simple solution, to take an either/or stance, and to deny mixed feelings.

Coping with the simultaneous existence of conflicting wishes —wanting to have your cake and eat it too—is one of life's major struggles. Regrettably, you rarely are in a position to have both. This is particularly true for the life-long conflict between the wish to be dependent and secure—to be taken care of and provided for—and the wish to be independent and autonomous—to do your own thing when and where you want. Much of the turmoil of adolescence stems from the shifting back and forth of this conflicting desire to be independent and still have the security of parental support and concern. Ambivalence is that state where one has mixed feelings but can only consciously acknowledge one set and must deny the contrary wish. Often, to maintain his self-esteem, the ambivalent adolescent has to deny any dependent wishes and act as if the only desire of any consequence is for independence. It is worth noting that in a good marriage, one may come the closest to satisfying the conflicting wishes for dependence and independence.

Not only can living be complicated by ambivalence, but also by resistance to change and a reluctance to face up to one's limits. Change is unsettling because it generally involves giving up something which is familiar and experiencing thereby a painful loss. Change also makes the world less predictable and secure, prompting uncertainty and anxiety. As a result, we tend to fight change and view it as a threat, even though mastering change may increase our sense of self-confidence and security. The reluctance to face limits also has roots in childhood. The infant perceives himself as *the* most important being in the world, to whom all should defer, and he may fantasize about being omnipotent. Growing up forces one to give up the fantasy of being all powerful, although we may continue to daydream of being Superman or Wonder Woman, of being a super athlete or president. Living forces a constant reassessment of one's limits and a realization that we may not even be as capable as some other people—people are not really created equal. The reassessment of one's own capacities and limits—physical, intellectual, emotional, occupational—is often painful, because we have to give up the fantasy of being able to do anything. Just as we seek to avoid painful situations, we often resist facing up to our limits and dealing with change. Yet one's capacity to make the most of living will generally reflect how he comes to grips with some of these basic principles of human behavior.

52

WHY THOSE NEW YEAR'S RESOLUTIONS FAIL

New Year's Day—the annual ringing in of the new. Time to forget the past and look ahead. Time for renewed hope and the traditional New Year's resolutions.

Yet, all too often, the resolutions don't last very long into the new year, despite the best of intentions. Somehow, something gets in the way, and the old temptations recur. Thus, you may be like the proverbial alcoholic who swears convincingly that he'll never take another drink and then goes out and gets drunk again.

Why? Simply stated, it's because we don't have as much control over ourselves as we think we do. "Hold on," you say. "That may be true for an alcoholic, but not for me. I've got will power." You do, until an emotional issue comes up. Then you're no different.

Sigmund Freud put it this way: "Students of human nature and philosophers have long taught us that we are mistaken in regarding our intelligence as an independent force, and in overlooking its dependence upon the emotional life. Our intelligence . . . can function reliably only when it is removed from the influences of strong emotional impulses; otherwise it behaves merely as an instrument of the will and delivers the inference which the will requires."

Freud was simply asserting a fact we don't like to acknowledge, that we are emotional animals, and we are not always fully aware of some emotions which are deeply buried within our personality and yet profoundly influence our behavior. Further, these powerful, motivating emotions are not particularly rational. Thus we can find ourselves doing things we can't readily explain. Like forgetting the name of someone we know very well just as we're introducing them to someone new. Or embarrassingly calling our wife by an old girl friend's name.

The human brain is a complex creation, with many levels of mental activity. It's much like an iceberg. There is much more mental activity going on beneath the surface, beyond our conscious awareness.

You meet someone new; and afterward you say, "I like that person." But you're not really sure why. Most likely, it is related to a host of factors you don't realize you noticed—appearance, manner, voice, gestures. Somewhere, positive associations were touched off in your mind, probably because the mannerisms were similar to some loved person in the past.

The old refrain of "I want a girl just like the girl that married dear old dad" touches on the same theme. It isn't just chance that you develop attachments to someone whose personality characteristics are similar to your parent of the opposite sex. Assuming you have positive memories of your mother/father, you've been programmed much like a computer to react positively when you meet a woman/man with similar characteristics.

This process takes place automatically, without any conscious deliberation. Indeed, while we may try to explain why we think, feel or act as we do, the significant reasons most often are buried in an unconscious part of our personality. The "unconscious" is a concept which many people don't like to accept. We don't like to admit we are not fully in control of ourselves, despite the fact we see evidence to the contrary in others repeatedly and, also, if we're honest, in ourselves.

So most of our conscious New Year's resolutions fail The wish to stop smoking or stop excessive drinking or stop being late is frustrated because there are stronger underlying emotional reasons for doing what we do. It takes more than just "will power" to counteract those reasons.

This isn't to say we can't get more control over ourselves. Indeed, there are plenty of instances where we can. But it first may be necessary to admit there is an adversary within the lines, a contrary opinion within. And we aren't as in charge of ourselves as we would like to think. Thus in the program of Alcoholics Anonymous, an important step is the alcoholic's admission that he cannot control the habit by will power alone.

The most important resolution for the New Year may well be to respect those emotional pressures within. They are formidable, and the challenge is to find new ways for you to control them, instead of being controlled by them.

ON THE EXPRESSION OF FEELINGS

A column on my son's experiences of giving flowers to others brought these responses:

Dear Dr. Menninger:
Thank you for your beautiful article on your "flower child." I would like to share an experience I had in the same field—giving flowers unexpectedly.

I work in my father's office and have been for six months. The women in the office were so sweet, obliging and oblivious to the fact that I was the boss's daughter; to this day, I can't get over my quick acceptance there.

At Easter, I wanted to do something special, so I asked my dad if I could get all four of them corsages. He immediately said yes.

Needless to say (and I'm sure your son could understand), they loved not only the flowers, but also the thoughts behind them. As you said, they are a symbol.

I will never forget the candid, almost childish smiles they brought, almost bringing tears to my eyes. Thanks again.
A. R.

Dear Dr. Menninger:
I was impressed to read the "Beauty of Flowers Speaks

*of Feelings." Could you please write more about how feel-
ings may be brought out into the open and shared with a
person.*

*I am also one who gives flowers in place of speaking
feelings to a person, which I often don't have the words to
do. There are many people, I assume, who would like to
read more about human beings' feelings in general.*

Sincerely,
M. H.

Feelings are fascinating, and often frightening. But feelings
are part-and-parcel of being human. They provide the spice in
life, both the bitter and the sweet. They can complicate life
immensely; but without them life would be a dull experience
indeed.

Feelings are hard to get out in the open and to share—at least
for adults, and adolescents too. Children can be openly affectionate or openly enraged, and we can still accept them. But in
grownups? Not usually.

Our culture puts special restraints on the expression of many
feelings, especially in men. It isn't manly to cry, or to be openly
affectionate, especially toward other men.

Yet, it isn't just the culture that prohibits open expression of
feelings. In the process of growing up, the child learns to put the
lid on feelings. Powerful inner feelings may lead to impulsive
behavior that has unfortunate results, so they must be controlled.

Normally, as you mature, you develop a repertoire of ways to
express feelings. Some do have a way with words and can articu-
late feelings so beautifully that others wish to use their words—
like Christian, who spoke to Roxanne wooing her through the

magnificent words of Cyrano de Bergerac. You may search in a similar way for the poem or greeting card to convey that special message to someone.

Feelings may also be conveyed through music or art or drama or dance. I'm repeatedly impressed by the feelings in the rock music of the younger generation. Or the power of dramatic expression in such plays as *1776* during the Bicentennial, or *Fiddler on the Roof,* or *Man of La Mancha.*

Individual actions may be quite effective in communicating feelings, as in the case of the flowers, or bonbons, or other gifts— "diamonds are forever." Or as in doing that little extra for someone you love, a special favor which you know will give the intended person a particular pleasure.

Of course, actions and words may convey negative as well as positive feelings. When feelings are mixed, the action-communication generally conveys the dominant feeling of the moment; that is, actions do speak louder than words.

It is easy to deny or fail to recognize the extent of mixed feelings in relationships. No matter how much you love someone, there are likely to be times when you are frustrated or angry toward that same person, and show it.

"HE NEVER SAYS 'I LOVE YOU'"

"He won't tell me he loves me any more."

These were the words of a young wife, married for six years to a rising young executive. She had called me for advice and was tearful and bitter as she spoke of the differences in the marriage.

I knew her to be a well-organized, loyal, dependable and competent woman. She had sacrificed to help her husband in his career, tailoring her own career to fit his needs during the early years of the marriage.

Her husband now was quite a success and well regarded by his peers. He was earning a comfortable income, too. In the process of doing well, he widened his circle of acquaintances. Along the way he met a most attractive woman, younger than his wife, who fawned over him and made him feel good.

His wife was more matter-of-fact. She felt that after the sacrifices and deprivation of the early years of marriage, they should now share the good times. But he wasn't interested in taking her out.

She was hurt when she learned of his affair with the other woman. But what hurt her most of all was the fact that "he's not sure if he loves me now, and he never says, 'I love you.'"

Those are precious words when said with feeling and genuine caring. They are much sought after as a sign of commitment. Yet what is love? Though the term is commonly used in every language, it is used in many different ways.

Some people have suggested that to examine love will destroy it. That position was attributed to Senator William Proxmire after he was critical of a government funded study to examine people falling in love. Since almost everyone experiences that, why should we need to study it? Primarily it is because we don't know as much about it as we think we do.

Of course, it has been studied. My uncle, Dr. Karl Menninger, in collaboration with his wife Jean, published a book on the subject over thirty years ago, *Love Against Hate.*

Love can be seen as a manifestation of the life instinct, but there are still many aspects of it which we do not understand. And there are different kinds of love, and sudden shifts of affection which people can experience without any apparent explanation.

If you look around, you have no trouble observing that different people have different patterns of love; and in any couple the pattern may change as life circumstances change. This was true for the young woman who called me. She was faced with reassessing the nature of the love she and her husband had in their relationship.

Many of the problems brought to marriage counselors have to do with different expectations of a husband and wife of their relationship and their different patterns of love.

What do you mean when you say, "I love you"?

One answer can be found in "I Love You But I'm Not in Love With You," a paper presented in 1975 to the American Association of Marriage and Family Counselors by Thomas and Marcia Lasswell. He is professor of sociology at the University of Southern California and she is professor of psychology at California State Polytechnic University at Pomona.

They were struck by how often people assume there is a popular, one-dimensional concept of love. From questioning more than one thousand subjects, they identified several types of love of one partner for another.

In addition to the familiar romantic type of love, they identified patterns of life-long friends, a totally forgiving love, a possessive love with intense dependency, logical-sensible love and the self-centered game-player love.

The Lasswells concluded that people are most likely to expect others to love them according to the meaning of love that they themselves have. And problems develop in a relationship when the definitions of the loving relationship are not in agreement for a couple.

WHAT MAKES YOU FALL IN LOVE?

What makes you fall in love with somebody? Why did you marry the person you did? What makes someone else attractive to you?

One of the earliest of Senator William Proxmire's "Golden Fleece" awards was given the government grant to do research on what makes people fall in love. He thought that was a stupid question to research.

Maybe it isn't important to know what attracts one person to another, but I think it is an intriguing question. And there are times when people become involved in relationships they can't explain, and which can be most embarrassing.

In an issue of Medical Aspects of Human Sexuality, a number of social scientists were queried about what they thought was involved in attractiveness in relationships.

A common underlying theme of the response was "our unconscious"—those feelings, preferences and desires which stem from earlier life experiences and which are buried in our mind beyond our conscious awareness.

Dr. Charles Wahl, clinical professor of psychiatry at UCLA put it this way: "While most persons can give glib and easy responses to such questions on why they married their particular spouse or prefer one physical or psychological type over another, the sum of clinical experience strongly supports the conviction that we do not leave our unconscious at home when we go spouse-hunting."

Wahl recalls the old song, "I Want a Girl Just Like the Girl that Married Dear Old Dad." That sentiment reflects the origin of nearly all sexual attraction—the force, direction and character of which come as a consequence of our first family attachments.

In his response, Dr. Bernard Murstein, professor of psychology at Connecticut College, discusses four contributing factors. Two of these are what he calls habituation and unconscious needs.

By habituation, Murstein refers to the physical impact of early loving parental figures. Thus, "a man who has a plump mother who was loving to him may tend to associate plumpness with a warm, nurturant personality and be attracted to that quality in women."

His unconscious needs explain attractions which seem to defy a person's logic, such as a woman being attracted to a cold, distant, sadistic man. Often, such a choice is an effort to "rectify certain unresolved childhood problems."

A woman who experienced her father as fearful, angry and distant in childhood may end up being attracted to a man in later life who recapitulates the emotional desertion she experienced from father.

In the context of her adult life, the choice may appear to be irrational. But unconsciously, if she can get this man to be attracted to her, she will have finally resolved the situation she could not satisfy with her real father.

Murstein's third element influencing attractiveness is the cultural stereotype of physical beauty and attractiveness, conveyed in movies and on television, etc.

Finally, there is the influence of what Murstein calls unattained ideals. One person may be attracted to another because of what the other may offer. A shy, inhibited man who wishes he were more assertive and outgoing may be attracted to an asserttive, open woman, from whose actions he achieves a vicarious satisfaction.

Actually, these social scientists all pretty much agreed that attractiveness often has surprisingly little to do with physique and appearance. As Murstein comments, "We generally respond to what we have learned to respond to or need to respond to."

EVEN THE STRONGEST PERSON CAN BREAK

Recently, I was asked to testify in a federal court trial on the impact of being put in prison. It is a stressful experience, certainly. How great a stress depends upon many factors, some within the individual, and some in the prison environment.

An interesting perspective on this question is found in a report from some Canadian behavior scientists who made a thirty-year follow-up study on some men who were prisoners of war in World War II. The study findings are also notable because of the fairly recent experience in this country with returned Vietnam POWs.

The Canadians studied a sample of eighty-seven survivors of imprisonment during World War II in either Germany or Japan. The individuals were examined with respect to their physical health, psychiatric condition and performance on psychological tests.

At the time of the follow-up study, all the subjects were functioning reasonably well and had no special problems. Their average age was fifty-six.

It is generally known that the conditions of the German POW camps were much better that those of the Japanese. The research investigators therefore compared the findings of the ex-German POWs and the ex-Japanese POWs; and they hypothesized that the veterans of the Japanese POW camps would show greater impairment, because they had a more stressful internment experience.

The two groups' backgrounds were roughly equivalent prior to the stressful experience in a POW camp. However, as the researchers anticipated, the high stress group—Japanese POWs—did show significantly more signs of psychiatric difficulty than the low stress group—German POWs.

Likewise, the physical health was worse for the high stress group, as was the impairment in psychological test performance. Further, there appeared to be a direct relationship between the residual effects and the duration of imprisonment. The longer a person had been a POW, the greater was his impairment thirty years later.

Persisting physical symptoms were primarily confined to the ex-Japanese POWs, who had many more neurological and muscular or joint problems. The findings suggested that the harsh conditions in the Japanese POW camps led to health problems.

The Canadian study makes clear that there are long-term, residual effects of the POW imprisonment. When the conditions of internment are harsh, the longer one is a prisoner, the more striking the long-term effects are.

A person who is physically strong and emotionally well adjusted will be able to stand a greater stress that one who is less strong. But even the strongest person has limits and will break under harsh circumstances. POW experiences in the Korean conflict as well as Vietnam have repeatedly demonstrated this point.

It is hard for anyone who has not gone through the stress of imprisonment to fully appreciate the readjustment necessary when a POW comes home. A few years ago, a number of returned Vietnam POWs experienced tragic personal failures to readjust back home.

There is a parallel in the POW experience to the experience of a repeated criminal offender in our society who spends a long period in prison. After a long prison term, the ex-convict may be quite limited in his ability to readjust to the "free world."

All too often, the free world is more obviously a cold, cruel world which drives the offender to commit another crime and be returned to the more familiar, predictable prison setting.

GOODNESS AND BADNESS—VIEWS OF BEHAVIOR

From the same community came these two letters, in response to my column discussing some aspects of homosexuality:

Dear Dr. Menninger:

Your answer to a woman's question about homosexuality was ridiculous!

It's evident you don't know very much about that, at least. Homosexuality is just one more indication of how sick our society is becoming. Living in such a state is each person's privilege, but having such immorality pushed on people who know what it really is, is very objectionable.

We're bombarded on every side, including television, to try to make it appear all right; but it is the basest kind of immorality. Too bad we don't have more people like Anita Bryant who are willing to stand for right.

Mrs. C. H.

Dear Dr. Menninger:

Thank you so much for your article. You said some of the things I have been wanting to say to a lot of people.

Our son is gay, and I know the misery and suffering he has been through because of what others say and do.

He sought help in a mental health clinic and even tried to end his life, to keep from hurting others in the family by

68

what people would say. But he found out we love him and
will stick by him.

No one knows how it hurts a gay person and their family
to have to listen to others make wisecracks and talk as if
they weren't human beings. God bless you for writing such
a fine article.

Sincerely,
Mr. and Mrs. W. H.

It is a troubling tendency of people to divide the world into *we*
and *they*. *We* are good and *they* are bad. *We* are right, and *they*
are wrong or immoral.

Of course, the truth is that both good and bad reside within
every individual. Therein lies the problem, for no one likes to
acknowledge the badness within. It is best to keep it private or
hidden, and to put one's best foot forward.

The struggle of coping with badness within oneself goes back
a long way, to that time when the young child comes to a stark
realization. Even though you may be a "good" boy or girl, there
is still "bad stuff" which comes out of you—namely, your "BM."
Our bowel movement is something to be treated with distaste
and disgust and eliminated privately.

Of course, to the adult mind this may seem silly. The body's
elimination of waste products through metabolism is a natural
process. but the developing child who is learning what life is all
about doesn't understand this. He simply learns that bad stuff
comes out—which obviously means there is something bad inside!

This potential "badness" is inside everyone all his or her life
and we cope with it in different ways, depending in part on the
messages we got as children, and how we were treated and

69

respected as a person.

Not many people consciously seek a "bad" identity, but some seem to. Certain youngsters get themselves fixed in a "bad" identity and act it out, getting attention and recognition by their bad behavior in school or at home, rather than being "good."

Most people want to be seen as good and behave accordingly. Others emphasize their goodness by contrasting themselves against the people who are worse in some way. Some are good by saving others who are bad.

It's so easy to be righteous and so hard to be tolerant and understanding. But tolerance means each must recognize that the potential for goodness and for badness exists in everyone!

"I WANT A GIRL, JUST LIKE THE GIRL . . ."

Dear Dr. Menninger:

I have recently read about the Oedipus Complex. I would appreciate receiving information about this theory in today's family relationship. Thank you.

Sincerely,
W. K.

You are perhaps aware that the Oedipus Complex was the term coined by Sigmund Freud to refer to a phase of personality development in childhood.

In his pyschoanalytic work, Freud was impressed by childhood wishes to displace the parent of the same sex, in order to have the total attention and concern of the parent of the opposite sex.

That wish called to Freud's mind the story of a hero in Greek mythology, Oedipus, who ended up killing his father and taking his mother for his wife.

Warned by Apollo that his own son would kill him, King Laius left the newborn Oedipus on a mountainside to die. Saved by a shepherd, Oedipus was adopted by a king in another country and grew up unaware of his true father and mother.

Later, traveling in the country of his birth, he unwittingly killed his father in a roadside argument. Then, after he rid the country of the Sphinx, he was made king and married the ex-king's widow, not realizing she was his mother, nor she knowing he was really her son.

In the normal growth and development of a youngster, around the age of four to seven, a child may openly express a strong preference for an exclusive relationship with the parent of the opposite sex. While it may go unnoticed if you are not looking for it, sometimes it is quite obvious.

The little boy may be delighted when daddy is off at work and he has mommy all to himself. Or the little girl pushes her mother away and plays up coquettishly to daddy and wants to do things with him alone. Often the youngster will climb into bed between the parents, literally separating them.

Some people were upset with Freud's ideas, interpreting the child's desires for a relationship in adult sexual terms. While young children may have some sense of adult sexual interaction, it is more reasonable to assume the child's wish is for a kind of total possession of the parent.

In a one-parent family, there are modifications to the struggle of the child; but in the normal family constellation, the child ultimately recognizes that he or she can't beat the competition. The other parent clearly has the inside track.

Further, the child may experience some underlying anxiety about what might happen if his or her wishes to eliminate the other parent might become known. So, the child gives up the immediate desires for the opposite-sex parent; and "if you can't beat 'em, join 'em!"

The child sets aside for the time being the selection of a mate and identifies with or strives to be like the parent of the same sex. For many people, the ultimate selection of a mate is still very much determined by the characteristics of the original opposite-sex parent.

You see this in most marriages, and it is reflected in "I Want a Girl, Just Like the Girl that Married Dear Old Dad."

The implications? Not really much different in today's family relationships than in the past. This is a part of life, a normal process through which every child passes, sorting out sexual relationships and figuring out one's own sexual identity and preferences.

VOLUNTARY SIMPLICITY—NOT JUST A FAD

Ever heard of Voluntary Simplicity? I hadn't until I came across an interesting publication called the *CoEvolution Quarterly.* In the Summer 1977, issue of that publication are several articles on Voluntary Simplicity.

What about Voluntary Simplicity? The phrase was coined by Richard Gregg in an article which appeared in an Indian journal in 1936. The term refers to a balance of one's inner attitude and way of living.

Wrote Gregg, "It means singleness of purpose, sincerity and honesty within, as well as avoidance of exterior clutter . . . a partial restraint in some directions in order to secure greater abundance of life in other directions."

The concept was picked up and restated in contemporary terms by a Stanford Research Institute study. Reporting to corporate subscribers of the Institute's Business Intelligence Program, SRI predicted that the fastest growing sector of the market is people committed to a lifestyle of voluntary simplicity.

The SRI researchers, Duane Elgin and Arnold Mitchell, consider the essence of voluntary simplicity to be "living in a way that is outwardly simple and inwardly rich."

The key values of the V/S movement are material simplicity, living and working in settings of a smaller, human scale, self-determination, ecological awareness, and personal growth.

The SRI study finds that voluntary simplicity is neither a back-to-nature movement, nor is it simply a "counterculture" as was prevalent in the 1960s. It is also not to be equated with living in poverty, or as being just a fad.

Rather, V/S appears to be a practical, workable and meaningful way of life for a small but significant segment of the population. Roughly two groups are identified as taking this direction.

One is composed of families or individuals who have voluntarily taken up a simple life after some years of involvement in the mainstream of society. The other group tends to be younger, more philosophically motivated, more activist, and more given to promoting the V/S view.

One form of the voluntary simplicity is in the so-called "Briarpatch Business." These are small businesses, individual firms working in such areas as food, clothing, restaurants, auto repair, baking, small-scale manufacture, etc.

The businesses are characterized by job-sharing and job-swapping; people fulfilling multiple jobs; people performing functions without titles; recycling surpluses; setting prices according to what you would charge your friends.

The SRI report concludes that the voluntary simplicity movement addresses some critical issues of our times—the problems of "ecosystem overload, alienation, unmanageable scale and complexity of institutions, worldwide antagonism, and so on."

Further, the lifestyle "meshes with the eternal needs of individuals to continue to grow. The emphasis on the inner life . . . permits people to grow psychologically even if material growth may be denied by events beyond their control."

A WOMAN'S PLACE IS . . . NOT IN ROTARY?

Perhaps I shouldn't be, but I continue to be impressed with the resistance of so many men to accept women on equal terms.

The last example was the Rotary International, which officially booted the Rotary Club of Duarte, California, out of the organization because the Duarte Chapter took in some women members.

The president of the Duarte Chapter, Dr. Richard Key, noted that two-thirds of the business and professional people in that city of sixteen thousand are women. Thus, "It's pretty rough to run a service organization for business and professional persons without letting women in these days."

But Rotary International is not for "persons." By its constitution, it is an international service organization of business and professional *men*. When that constitution was formulated in the early 1930s, that made sense. But today?

What really is more important to Rotary? Maintaining an exclusive organization for men; or being committed to fulfill the significant objectives also outlined in the Rotary constitution— encouraging ideals of service; recognizing the worthiness of all useful occupations; advancing international understanding, goodwill and peace through world fellowship?

I have been a Rotarian and I have appreciated recognition which my local club has awarded me. I also respect the statement of principles in which Rotary places great store, their "Four-Way Test":

1. Is it the truth?
2. Is it fair to all concerned?
3. Will it build good will and better relationships?
4. Will it be beneficial to all concerned?

It seems a bit inconsistent for Rotary to espouse such noble principles for its membership and then to disavow a club which has accepted women into the organization to fulfill Rotarian objectives.

Why does this nonsense occur? Defenders of tradition may offer various rationalizations, but when you get to the bottom line, it's because that's the way it has always been. Change is unsettling, especially when the change involves a new perception of the traditional roles of men and women.

Any change makes life less predictable. You can learn from experience only when the world is stable and consistent. If things are constantly changing, you are at a loss to predict what will happen and know what to do next.

English social scientist Peter Marris has made these points well in his book *Loss and Change* (Anchor Books).

Marris observes that we cannot act without some interpretation which makes sense of what is going on about us. To make an interpretation, we must first match our current experience with some familiar previous experience.

Anything which threatens to invalidate the way we understand the world around us is disruptive. And we may act like the computer which responds, "That does not compute!"

Marris suggests that the "impulses of conservatism" defend our ability to make sense out of life. These impulses are: "to ignore or avoid events which do not match our understanding;

to control deviation for expected behavior; to isolate innovation and sustain the segregation of different aspects of life."

A Rotary Club with women is certainly not the model with which most Rotarian leaders have grown up. A woman's place is in the home; that was the way it was for most middle-aged people.

It is still hard for many men in positions of leadership to realize how much the role of women has changed. Today, for the majority of American women, their place is at work, as well as home. And women are perfectly able to assume responsible positions in business and professional work.

Rotary International is living in the past. If they're truly committed to the four-way test, they'd better change their constitution to make way for women. And give credit to Duarte for sustaining its commitment to the important Rotarian ideals.

PART THREE

Hazards

A golf course has a number of hazards, both natural and artificial—the rough bordering the fairways, streams and ponds between the tee and the hole, and sand traps protecting the greens. These hazards are generally designed so as to make the course more interesting and more challenging to the golfer; on a competitive course, they also serve to separate the good golfers from those who are less talented. While one may emphasize these well-defined physical hazards which affect the game of golf, the actual play of the golfer is influenced as much or more by other factors which are equally hazardous to his successful play. These factors include the character and skill of the golfer himself and the driving forces within him, the state of his physical and mental health, the worries he has about other things going on in his life which he can't put out of his mind.

On the golf course, the physical hazards serve to do more than complicate the golfer's life and increase the difficulty of his play. They may prompt him to improve his skills and sharpen his game more than if he were to play on a course with wide fairways and few bunkers. When your ball lands in a sand trap, it can be most frustrating. But unless you have some experience in that position, you may not develop any skill for getting out of such a jam. In the same way, hazards in life, though frustrating and painful, can have a positive side. A certain amount of stress is necessary to challenge one to grow and develop and increase one's mastery in life. Most educators realize that an optimal amount of anxiety is necessary to stimulate students to learn; and one of the functions of examinations is to force the student to review his material and reinforce the learning process. There is value in being tempered by adversity and by experiencing an optimum of frustration and failure. The key to having such an experience be beneficial is that the stress be sufficient to stimulate growth but not so great as to overwhelm or devastate.

In life, as in the game of golf, the hazards or stresses exist both within the individual player and outside on the "course." Some are natural; some are artificially created. Some are obvious; some are hidden. One may tend to focus on the external hazards since they are usually more obvious than the internal. Further, if our psychological defenses are working effectively, we blind ourselves to some of our inner conflicts and weaknesses. Nonetheless, the inner hazards may be far and away the most significant influence upon one's adjustment in life.

What are some of these inner hazards? Emotions head the list. Our feelings provide the flavor in life, the spice which makes life exciting and thrilling and joyful . . . and sad and discouraging and enraging. For the most part, our emotions are what complicate our relationships with other people; without them, we might get along quite well with one another. But how dull life would be without feeling. Actually, some of life's greatest pleasures are associated with the release of feeling or the free experience of emotions; at the same time, some of life's painful moments may result from the loss of control of emotions.

Of the dominant emotional experiences of love and hate, our culture seems to be more comfortable with the expression of aggression than of affection. There are those people who seem to be so threatened by the expression of any intense feeling that they attempt to repress all emotions. Many people, however, find it easier to express anger and resentment than love and affection, perhaps because the sexual drive is such a powerful inner force. Certainly, sexual impulses and sexual behavior are most troublesome to many people, and exposing such feelings presents special hazards. It's not "proper" to be too interested in sex, so that interest has to be disguised or denied. Its strong existence is demonstrated by the financial success of the sexually-oriented magazines in this country; and more than one editor acknowledged an interest in my syndicated feature "In-Sights" because it would periodically deal with sexual concerns in a manner acceptable to the daily newspaper.

In addition to emotional drives, there are other internal stresses. One's physical and mental health often reflect a capacity to adapt in life; ill health can signal a failure to master some life situation. Illness can also become an additional stress. In any case, it behooves everyone to respect the message to yourself when your body or your mind gives evidence of malfunction.

For some people, being different poses a special stress. That difference may be obvious to others—a difference in sex, in color, in religion—or not. Many people dwell on inner fears or feelings of being different which are well concealed. When you are different, you are vulnerable to being put down or rejected by others, often as a result of an irrational prejudice.

As one grows older in life, there are stresses which result from the process of aging—the change of life (menopause), the change of expectations in life (midlife crisis), diminishing capacity, anticipating retirement, and the prospect of death.

Man is a social animal. Thus, most people derive their greatest pleasure from relationships with others. The positive feedback of love and affection and praise which we get from others helps to sustain us in our travail through life. From that interaction, we achieve a sense of value and meaning and satisfaction. But those relationships cut both ways, so that other people are also responsible for a great deal of our stress in life—when they criticize us, hurt us, reject us, frustrate us. Of course, sometimes we deserve what we get in the way of pain by creating problems with others by our behavior. In any case, the most significant external hazards in life are not the natural catastrophes of flood, famine, fire, earthquake, etc. Rather, they are the result of problems in getting along with other people—people in general, our life's companion, our children.

Coupling through marriage is the predominant pattern of living in our society. Yet, the past several decades have seen an easing of the permanence of that coupling. An increased incidence of living-together arrangements and of divorce have suggested to some that marriage may be out of style, and that the marital contract presents too many hazards to be sustained. However, those persons who have achieved a successful marriage find through sharing life's stresses, they have a greater strength and they also achieve greater satisfactions.

One of the products of marriage is the perpetuation of the race and the society, in the form of children. But raising children presents a whole new set of hazards. Our society does not educate adults to be parents in any systematic and effective manner. Rather, one tends to learn from the experience of having children, which can be most traumatic. Many search for guidebooks —the wisdom of Dr. Spock or Haim Ginot—in hopes of properly raising these young creatures in the best way. Many parents doubt their own common sense about childrearing, and are constantly torn between a vicarious pride in a youngster's accomplishment and a deep sense of failure when a child's behavior is embarrassing. Parents struggle with a sense of responsibility for their children, balancing a proprietary interest in the child with an awareness that he or she ultimately grows into an independent human being with a separate life to lead.

Parents often experience an intense desire to keep their children from having the unhappy experiences they had. Yet, it is impossible to prevent our children from having their own disappointments, hurts, or deprivation. That is the nature of life. Try as one might, the parent cannot really "do it" for his children, no more than our parents could do it for us.

The essays which follow in this section elaborate upon some of the foregoing stresses—internal and external—which make living hazardous.

STRESS—NOT ONLY NORMAL, BUT ESSENTIAL

Not long ago, I heard a sermon make reference to one of the most important four-letter words in the English language—"cope." And coping with stress is a struggle for everyone.

In one form or another, I get asked more questions about coping with stress than any other topic. Whether a housewife or an office worker, a student or an executive, you encounter stress. What do you do about it?

The Blue Cross Association is concerned about what you do about it, because they operate the largest hospital insurance program in the nation. So they called on a number of specialists to write about coping with stress and have published their articles in a ninety-six page booklet.

In his introduction, Walter J. McNerney, president of the Blue Cross Association, indicates that the booklet was prepared for the layman, the working man or woman, persons of all ages who want to learn more about stress and its effect on health and happiness.

The articles are written in a readable and easily understood style. Some sample observations:

Psychiatrist Donald Oken authors an overview of stress and notes, "We often tend to think of stress as harmful—an enemy of health. In fact, the stress response is not only normal, but essential. Without it, we could not live very long."

Oken goes on to suggest that if you can learn to deal with stress and master it, stress can make you stronger; your capacity to remain healthy will be enhanced. But if you fail to find effective solutions, stress will increase and take its toll in a physical or mental breakdown.

Pediatric Psychologist Lee Salk talks about what parents can do to help children: "Being consistent and enforcing rules is not only a way of helping children cope with stress and build self-control, but it is a way parents have of showing love and concern for their child."

Psychiatrist Robert Coles on adolescence and what parents must realize: "Often it is a matter of knowing how to keep one's distance, of being there without being especially insistent or inquisitive."

Dr. James Birren on middle-age stress: "A common situation of the working person is that he or she has too much to do and not enough time to do everything. He or she is experiencing an 'overload.'

"Successful middle-aged people seem to know when to pull back. They have learned the signs that tell them they are in over their heads—the headache; the inability to sleep well; nothing looks good to eat, or everything does; every little thing is irritating."

Dr. Ralph Collins, for twenty-five years a staff psychiatrist for the Eastman Kodak Company:

"Each of us needs an outlet for pent-up emotions of anger, frustration, hostility and discouragement which develop from life's situations. Too often, ill feelings are passed along in epidemic fashion . . .

"We should all choose some safety valve activity, be it a sport, hobby, music, reading, or even just a long relaxing walk to cool off after a harder than usual day at work."

Gerald Caplan, professor of psychiatry at Harvard: "We have seen how people in crisis can be helped to become more comfortable and effective if given the active support and guidance of relatives, friends and neighbors, and of professionals such as clergymen, physicians, nurses, social workers and teachers."

I happened to pick up a copy of this booklet, *Stress,* in the office of a family practitioner. If you are interested in getting a copy, contact your local Blue Cross Plan office. Or you may write the Office of Public Relations, Blue Cross Association, 840 North Lake Shore Drive, Chicago, Illinois 60611.

WHAT CAN HELP SELF-CONFIDENCE?

Dear Dr. Menninger:

I am a man around fifty years of age; and most of my life, I have lacked confidence in myself. I am also very sensitive.

I try every now and then to get rid of my sensitivity and lack of self-confidence, but I do not seem to be able to conquer both these faults. I would appreciate your help with this problem.

Sincerely,
R. S., Sacramento

You may feel you are alone in experiencing problems with self-confidence and sensitivity. But you are not. These two personal characteristics are not always easy to keep in proper balance.

Even someone who seems strong and healthy in every way can have periods of doubt about what he is doing. Or he can be deeply hurt by the comments or actions of others.

Of course, though we may like to think that all men (and women) are created equal, that is not true. There are real differences in natural abilities for intelligence, strength, talent, sensitivity, etc.

Throughout life, you have opportunities to develop and test your potentials; but the early life experiences do significantly influence later attitudes.

Take self-confidence. Obviously, your natural abilities will influence your confidence in yourself, but there's more to it than that. Your sense of being "good" and capable will be affected by how your parents treated you—whether they encouraged you or discouraged you as you grew up.

Further, you will be influenced by the kinds of experiences you had in school. In that setting, children inevitably compare their skills with those of their peers. If you didn't do as well, it's harder to sustain your self-confidence. If you were a late developer in adolescence, you could have a continuing sense of inferiority which is hard to overcome.

Hopefully, by the time one reaches adult years, you have a realistic idea of your abilities and can find the right niche to achieve some success and happiness. But even people who are extremely talented can be lonely and unhappy and filled with self-doubt.

I have repeatedly been impressed by the unseen side of some highly successful people who appear to outsiders to be supremely self-confident and on top of the world.

Strange as it may seem, beneath the veneer of that confidence are so many doubts that the person must surround himself with "yes" men to be constantly reassured of his success. Even presidents have been filled with such doubt and insecurity.

With regard to your sensitivity, either extreme is undesirable. Insensitive people can be obnoxious and a pain to others. Hypersensitive people may hurt constantly from the slights or personal rejections from others.

Some people who find relationships too painful simply withdraw and avoid contact with others. Some cover their sensitivity with an outward "gruffness"—the best defense is a good offense

—to keep people at a distance. Yet others blot out the pain by "anesthetizing" themselves with alcohol or drugs.

Preoccupied with your own struggles, you may not sense how much you have in common with others. But the sales of self-help books point to the widespread lack of confidence in people.

Such books may be one source to help to you. In this field, I continue to be impressed with a bestseller of some years back, *"I'm O.K., You're O.K.,"* by Dr. Thomas Harris.

Also, you may get help through participation in a group experience. There are some educational classes which may give you some confidence—Dale Carnegie courses, night school and church classes in self-awareness and the like. Or you may join a group which is frankly therapeutic, sponsored by a mental health center or pyschiatric clinic.

Internal Stress: Sex

IS THERE A NEW MORALITY

The woman was obviously worried. She was middle-aged and worked fulltime. She has a teenaged daughter. She was asking if I thought there really was a new morality regarding sexual behavior.

As she spoke, I recalled one wag's definition of a sexual conservative: a liberal with a sixteen-year-old daughter!

What do you mean by morality? Is it attitude or behavior? And when you ask about something new, compared to what? Prior to Kinsey's landmark surveys, there were few studies which provided any baseline data for comparison. And even Kinsey's work had its limitations. His sampling was not perfectly representative of the American public. He did, however, make people aware of facts about human sexual practices.

Until recently, most social scientists doubted that there was really a changed or "new" morality. They believed that people were simply more open and talked more freely about their sexual behavior. They did not find clear evidence that practices were changing.

Now, surveys of older people find little change from traditional and conservative attitudes and behavior about sex. At the same time, there is increasing evidence that young people are reflecting a new, more permissive attitude in their sexual behavior. Young people are, as a whole, sexually more liberated.

This trend is perhaps best illustrated in attitudes about a subject like pre-marital sexual intercourse. Back in 1937, a Roper Poll found roughly one in five respondents (22 percent) who thought premarital intercourse was all right for men and women; another 8 percent thought it was all right for men only; over half thought it was never right. The same inquiry by the Roper pollsters in 1959 got the same response pattern.

The Gallup Poll took a crack at the question in 1969, at which time two-thirds (68 percent) of the respondents still said that premarital sex was wrong. By 1973, less than half (48 percent) were saying it was wrong. The major change, however, came in the younger age group; a large majority of persons over age thirty still thought it was wrong. College students approved of it by a two-to-one ratio.

A *Playboy* survey in 1973 found over half the men (59 percent) and nearly half the women (43 percent) agreed with the statement, "People who have sex before marriage are more likely to have happy and stable marriages later on."

But these are just attitudes, you say. What about behavior? People haven't really changed have they? They're just talking more . . . ? Well, the Kinsey survey was an eye-opener because he found half of all the women in his sample had sexual intercourse before marriage, and the rate was even higher among the males.

Kantner and Zelnik reported in 1971 that better than one-fourth (28 percent) of never-married women ages fifteen to nineteen have had some coital experience. They found intercourse was beginning at younger ages and its extent among teenagers was increasing. And the *Playboy* survey found the percentage of married persons who had sexual intercourse prior to marriage was now 95 percent for males and 85 percent for females in the eighteen to twenty-four age range.

The evidence points to a marked shift toward greater openness and permissiveness in both sexual attitudes and behavior in the American population. This is particularly true for youth, but it is evident in all age groups.

One of the polls approaches this question from a different angle—the perspective of doctors. The *American Medical News* —the weekly newspaper published by the AMA—surveyed a nationwide sample of primary care physicians about how the sexual revolution had affected their practice. Doctors queried included general and family practitioners, internists, obstetrician/gynecologists and pediatricians.

Two-thirds of the doctors responding (65.3 percent) reported that the changes in attitudes toward sex were markedly reflected in their clinical practice. One-fourth—24 percent—denied seeing any signs of the sexual revolution in their practice, and the remainder—10.7 percent—couldn't say.

How did the two-thirds see changes? They had more requests for birth control information and more abortion information. They noted a higher incidence of venereal disease and related clinical problems—inflammations of the female genital organs. They cited more illegitimate births.

Internists note more inquiries about sex after a heart attack. Pediatricians report teenagers request sex counseling more frequently and are less reluctant to be examined than in the past. Ob/gyn specialists have more requests for sterilizations.

Patients are requesting help—counseling—for sexual problems more frequently than in the past. And a sizeable number of the physicians (74.2 percent) believe that patients today are more willing to openly discuss sexual problems than they were ten to fifteen years ago.

Are the physicians prepared to deal with the fallout from the sexual revolution in their practice on a day-to-day basis? Only one in four surveyed (26.4 percent) thought so; and more often, those were younger physicians.

Of course, like everyone else, physicians have their personal opinions about the changes in sex attitudes and behavior. Some view the trend positively, some negatively; few deny there has been a change.

Some of the positive comments: "It's a good thing." "Healthy." "An overdue adjustment to sexual reality." "A very significant advance in social maturation." "Progress toward a more natural, normal life." "The openness and willingness to discuss sexual problems is good."

On the negative side: "A breakdown of values." "It's a serious mistake that has shaken the whole moral fiber of the nation." "It has appreciably increased venereal disease and disrupted the family complex." "Tragic." "Disgusting." "A bummer."

Noted one doctor, on balance, "My old-fashioned, rigid thoughts are offended. But what's happening is probably a healthy sign for the future."

SEXUAL PROBLEMS RESULT
FROM POOR COMMUNICATION

Few couples manage to avoid having problems in their sexual relationship.

Sometimes, one partner has a so-called sexual dysfunction which impairs the relationship—impotence, pain on intercourse, premature ejaculation. Sometimes, it is a matter of dissatisfaction by one or both partners with the frequency or quality of the love-making.

Some people are neither "dysfunctional" nor dissatisfied, but are simply ignorant of the possibilities available to them.

For all of the above, and particularly the last group, the major problem may be one of communication—being unable to share feelings and desires effectively with your partner.

Dr. Allen Fay, a New York psychiatrist affiliated with the Mt. Sinai School of Medicine, believes that most communication problems result from difficulty with assertiveness.

He defines assertiveness as the capacity to make honest, direct, open and disclosing statements, both positive and negative, to other people; and to take action in one's best interests without putting others down or infringing on their rights. This includes the capacity to ask for what one wants and to refuse unreasonable requests.

In the sexual area, assertiveness involves the capacity to initiate love-making, to accept an overture, to decline an unwelcome advance, to express one's likes and dislikes about love-making, and to share fantasies and other intimate feelings.

Notes Fay, assertive people take steps to get what they want, although they recognize that their actions will not always be successful.

With regard to saying "no," especially to a loved one, it is important to be sympathetic to the other person's position and to indicate an ongoing interest. Suggests Fay, in general, when saying "no," it is better to express what you would like, rather than what you don't want; for example, "Let's do it tomorrow when I'm not so exhausted."

Dr. Fay calls attention to some of the more common and most destructive habits which impair communications and sexual satisfaction:

1. Inattentiveness and lack of overt expression of interest in what the other person is saying—the situation where one partner is so preoccupied with his or her own activities, he or she fails to be sensitive to the feelings and message of the partner.

2. Bringing up past grievances—reciting past errors, misdeeds and dissatisfactions tends to destroy, rather than enhance, a relationship.

3. Malignant hypotheses—drawing the wrong conclusion from a partner's behavior, like feeling the partner is unhappy or angry with you if he or she doesn't go along with what you want. (Fay urges people to be alert to this trap, to think of alternative explanations for the behavior and to ask the person directly for some clarification.)

4. Insufficient positive reinforcement—the tendency to criticize your partner for things you don't like, rather than telling him what you do like and what he does that pleases you.

5. Labeling the other person—fixing your partner into a "sex

maniac," a "pervert," or a "frigid woman."

6. Universalizing your own values and tastes—taking your views about sexual behavior or a given sexual practice to be "right" and "good," and assuming any other practice is automatically "bad."

7. Using absolutes—like saying "We *never* go out any more," or "We *always* make love the same way" in a critical manner; leave room for your partner to have an "out."

8. "You" messages—negative feelings are more apt to be destructive in a relationship if they start with "you" instead of "I." (Observes Fay, "You don't love me" is an accusation. "I feel unloved by you" is a statement of feeling.)

9. Self-justification—blaming things that go wrong on the partner and failing to look first at how "I" am contributing to the disharmony or what can "I" do to improve the situation.

COPING WITH SEX—KNOWLEDGE
SHOULD BE OUR ALLY

Dear Dr. Menninger:

*In a column on "Where Should We Learn About Sex,"
you stressed the importance of parents as a very important
source of information when enlightening children on sexual
matters.*

*I think most parents are tongue-tied when one of their
children asks about sex. It seems most parents do not
know how to approach such matters.*

*I agree that certain myths and stories surrounding sex
persist, because we get distorted ideas in our childhood
about sex—like playing "doctor" and getting scolded for it.
Or being told that you are not supposed to play with
yourself or terrible things will happen to you.*

*I guess the most significant statement you made is that
"knowledge should be our ally in managing that force (sex)
in life, so that it does not manage us." So it is very important
that we sort out the facts from the myths in teaching
our children about sex.*

Sincerely,
E. S.

Your words, E. S., are true. Parents should know the facts to be
able to share the information with their children. Two good

source books on the subject are *Fundamentals of Human Sexuality* by Herant Katchadourian and Donald Lunde (Holt, Rinehart & Winston, New York, 1975, Second Edition), and *Human Sexualities* by John Gagnon (Scott Foresman & Co, Glenview, IL, 1977).

Wardell Pomeroy, who was associated with Dr. Kinsey, has written books for pre- or early-adolescent youngsters: *Boys and Sex* and *Girls and Sex* (Delacorte Press, New York, 1968). Each has a special introduction for parents.

Another letter shares some feelings about the consequences as a youngster of not having learned about sex:

Dear Dr. Menninger:

I read your article on pregnant teenagers and want to share my experience. I attended a Catholic school. As far back as I can remember, sex was a mortal sin to even think about.

From an early age, I wondered about sex, but it was put in a closet and no one talked about it. As I began to experience sexual feelings, I had no idea what I was supposed to do, except ignore them! But I was confused.

I never had a birds-and-bees talk from my parents— they were too embarrassed. My school didn't believe in teaching a sex class. I did have a marriage class, but the priest started at the point where "the woman was nine months along, and her husband came home drunk and started beating her." Some marriage course.

Like many of my friends, I didn't start dating until my sophomore year in high school. I had few boy friends, but I did experience some intense feelings of sexual arousal. I did have morals, and there were only two boys with whom

I felt close enough to do more than kiss.

I knew somehow I could get pregnant, but I honestly had no knowledge of conception or any way to prevent it. All I knew was that I cared very much for these two boys and I eventually married one of them.

What I'm saying is that there are many girls like myself who end up pregnant because we are not taught otherwise. Sure, we're told not to, but if a little reasoning were to go along with that command, we might think harder on the decision.

If we could sit down with our children and explain the difference between making love and having sex; if we could introduce them to their bodies and the functions of each organ; and if we could suggest ways to control them, they might be inclined to weigh all this information before saying yes or no.

Our government should allow more money to our schools for sex education and take it away from welfare. I have friends who have had three, four or five abortions; and welfare paid the whole tab. They know it will do so, so they don't bother too much with precautions.

Sincerely,
H. M.

SEX IS A CLOSED TOPIC

By the time a youngster reaches the age of sixteen, sex is a closed topic between him or her and parents. Adolescents guard their privacy in this area, and on the whole parents respect that privacy.

This was one of the findings of a thorough study of some eighty youngsters and their parents reported by Dr. Stella Chess, Dr. Alexander Thomas and Martha Cameron, all of the department of psychiatry at the New York University Medical Center.

They interviewed adolescents and their parents who were part of a longitudinal study in New York. The youngsters had actually been studied since early infancy, and were all from the middle-class, living in urban or suburban settings.

With regard to the communication about sex between generations, there was little discussion between adolescents and their parents about actual sexual behavior, in spite of changing sex mores in recent years, and in spite of liberal attitudes of many parents and their youngsters.

The parents had a general notion of the extent of their youngsters' sexual activity, and in most cases their assumptions appeared to be correct. Yet parents did not initiate discussions with their children about such matters as birth control, pregnancy, abortion or venereal disease.

In addition, with few exceptions, the parents in this study did not try to impose their own ethical values on their children. They viewed their children's behavior with mixed feelings, but were generally willing to respect the adolescent's judgment.

What about the youngsters' attitudes and behavior? With all the talk about the "revolution" in sexual attitudes of young people, it is refreshing to learn where these kids were at.

The advent of the pill has led many people to assume adolescents will be more sexually promiscuous. Such was not the case with this population. They were not prone to casual sexual encounters.

It is true that as a group they did not manifest the concerns of earlier generations about sex. For instance, worries about pregnancy, birth control, masturbation and venereal disease were not mentioned by the adolescents in the interviews. Their attitude toward these subjects was casual and matter-of-fact.

Also, they reflected little moral conflict or guilt about sex. Where conflict did exist, it appeared to be more a part of a parent-child relationship than guilt about sex in and of itself. A few youngsters who expressed a great deal of conflict in the area of sex presented evidence of severe emotional problems in other areas, too.

In their behavior, these youngsters paralleled a similar study where 10 percent of the adolescents had sexual intercourse by the end of their junior year of high school. By the end of the first year after high school, 30 percent had intercourse, and 50 percent had by the end of the third year after high school.

One other interesting sidelight: Although only a small number of girls stated that they were interested in women's liberation, the impact of the movement was clearly evident. When asked about their plans, very few of the girls mentioned marriage, and almost all of them had quite concrete career goals.

PREPARING A DAUGHTER FOR SEX

Dear Dr. Menninger:

My husband and I are not sure what to do.

We have a daughter who will soon graduate from high school and go off to college. She has been going steady with a young man for several months.

For the past few weeks, she has been on edge and easily upset. We thought it might be the prospect of graduation. But the other day, while putting away some clean clothes in her dresser, I noticed a letter on the bureau.

I know I shouldn't have looked at it, but I did. It was a letter from her boyfriend, which said he would stand by and marry her, if she is really pregnant.

That was a shocker! We realize, of course, that she is old enough for sex; but somehow we weren't really ready for it. I discussed it with my husband—who said I shouldn't have been so nosy—and we agreed I should talk the situation over with her.

When I did so, she actually seemed a bit relieved. (In retrospect, I suspect she really wanted me to discover and read the letter. It's as if she wanted us to know, but didn't know how to tell us.) She now knows she is not pregnant. But she still loves the boy and implies she will have sex with him again.

Of course, as a parent, I know that if my daughter wants to have sex, there's little I can do about that. But if she does, I would like to be sure she does so sensibly and does not get pregnant. Will advising her about a contraceptive just encourage her to have sex?

Sincerely,
Mrs. R. L.

There are few issues more emotionally laden than the sexual maturation and initiation of one's own children, especially a daughter. (Sons are expected to be sexually active; daughters are supposed to be protected and pure.)

You are right to be realistic and face up to your limitations in controlling your daughter's sexual activity. If your value system has not been conveyed to her by this time, it's too late. However, it is not too late to make sure she is fortified with knowledge about sex and contraception.

Of the twenty-one million young people in this country between fifteen and nineteen, more than half are estimated to have had sexual intercourse. In one survey of college students, two-thirds of the women and nearly three-fourths of the men acknowledged having had sexual intercourse. Of these men and women, 65 percent had their first intercourse at age eighteen or younger.

One additional finding of that study, which parallels the experience of your daughter, is that most young people engage in their first intercourse under conditions of high pregnancy risk. For seven out of ten young people, the first intercourse is not planned, usually because it is not expected at the time it happens. Where there is no planning, there is no contraceptive preparation.

An unplanned pregnancy can be an extremely disruptive event in a young person's life. Parents should assume a responsibility for preparing their children for the likelihood of sexual intercourse at some time, and for preparing the child to have that experience with the least risk to his or her future.

Preparing your daughter (or son) for that event should not be interpreted as encouraging its occurrence, if you present the information matter-of-factly. If your own value system is clear, your child will put this information in a proper perspective.

Be reassured by another finding in the college survey. While a majority of college students appear to engage in premarital intercourse, there is little evidence to suggest the majority are promiscuous. On the contrary, the experience of most is with only one partner.

THE PILL—OR NOT THE PILL?

Dear Dr. Menninger:
My eighteen-year old daughter is a senior in high school, and she has asked me about taking the pill. I have been on the pill for a number of years to avoid having more children. But I have heard that there is a higher death rate for women who have taken the pill.

I'm not sure what to tell my daughter, nor am I sure what to do myself. I can see all kinds of problems almost any way I go. Have you any suggestions?
Mrs. R. S.

You have lots of company. Increasingly, women are having second thoughts about taking the pill—the oral contraceptive—indefinitely.

There have been a good number of reports in the medical literature of higher death rates in women who have been on the pill. A recent British report found the death rate from circulatory system diseases to be five times greater in women who had used oral contraceptives than those who had not.

In women who had taken the pill continuously for five years or more, the mortality rate was ten times the control group. Further, the excess mortality went up with age, cigarette smoking and the duration of contraceptive use.

To anyone on the pill or considering taking it, these data are unsettling. Even though the actual death rate is still relatively low—another study found just nine cardiovascular deaths in 46,681 woman-years of pill use—the trend is undeniable.

In some ways, the dilemma of using the pill parallels the dilemma of the smoker. Like the smoker, the woman who takes the pill is concerned about a present anxiety or stress—in her case, avoiding pregnancy. She does not think about a remote consequence of an earlier future death.

Of course, there are other ways to achieve a freedom to engage in sex without fear of pregnancy. But all approaches to contraception have one or another limitation.

For example, consider the diaphragm. In combination with a spermicidal cream, that contraceptive technique is almost as effective as the pill. Yet many people resist using it. Why? There may be several reasons.

First, using the diaphragm is not as neat and clean as using the pill. To be completely effective, it requires some training, some advance preparation and some manipulation.

Second, insertion of the diaphragm involves physical contact with the genital area, a part of the body subject to childhood "taboos," which you're not supposed to "touch." It's also a part of the body about which many women and most men are quite ignorant.

Third, because it takes time and intent to prepare the diaphragm, its use makes the act of love more deliberate and less "impulsive." If you already feel some underlying guilt with the sexual act, being deliberate about it only increases that sense of guilt.

One way or another, there's obviously a "price" to be paid for sexual activity. Over the ages, the woman has pretty consistently had to pay that price—the man generally gets off scot-free.

I suppose there are those persons who believe if you want to be free and impulsive with sex, you ought to pay some price for it. They might not believe that the price should be an earlier death for some women, but it's clear that for those who use the pill, that may be the case!

Another solution is to help people to be more accepting of and responsible for their sexual impulses—not in a way that encourages promiscuity, but that reduces excessive guilt and allows reasonable, appropriate and safe contraceptive techniques to be utilized.

ABORTION CAN MEAN HAPPINESS AND RELIEF

The abortion issue has been on the front rank of issues in the current political scene. Most visible have been the outspoken anti-abortion opinions of those in the Right to Life Movement. For many, it is easy to speak out against abortion with righteous indignation and moral concern.

What is not heard are the reaction of women who have faced the dilemma of an unwanted pregnancy and opted for an abortion. There are a substantial number of women who have done so, but who do not feel comfortable speaking out.

The actual number of women in this group is not easily determined. The latest figures on abortion available from the U.S. Public Health Service indicate more than three-quarter million abortions were performed in 1974. Because many states provide incomplete or no information on abortions to the Public Health Service, the total reported is only a minimum figure.

Clearly, a great many women avail themselves of the procedure each year in this country. How do they feel about it? Researcher Nancy Adler, now with the University of California at Santa Cruz, sought the answer to that question by interviewing one hundred women in Boston who had abortions.

What did she find? Positive emotions are experienced most strongly. Indeed, the women widely share a sense of happiness and relief following abortion. In addition, a number of women

110

also experience some degree of negative feelings.

The degree of negative emotions which any one woman experienced was related sometimes to external factors, and sometimes to inner, personal factors. For example, a woman who was certain she did not want to continue her pregnancy would have few doubts or regrets afterward, but might still feel guilt, shame, and fear of disapproval if people near her felt that abortion was wrong. This was particularly true for women who were young, unmarried and involved in church activities.

Similarly, a woman whose social environment was favorable to abortion might not experience these emotions, but could experience a sense of loss and depression if she, in part, did want to be pregnant and have a child. That is, for some women, the pregnancy fulfills conscious or unconscious needs or desires. The woman may recognize that it was more desirable to terminate the pregnancy, but feels a sense of loss and regret nonetheless.

Another set of reactions to abortion is reported by a study of adolescent pregnancies by researcher Sherry Hatcher. The late adolescents she studied were "quite convinced that abortion laws should allow anyone to obtain a legal and safe termination of pregnancy on request."

Many of these girls emphasized that when they were younger they thought abortion to be an ugly, unforgivable act. But in the light of their own experiences with illegitimate pregnancy, they changed their minds.

It is significant that in both of these studies, where women were approached in a one-to-one interview setting, they expressed generally positive views about their abortions. As a psychiatrist who has interviewed both adolescent and older women troubled with an unwanted pregnancy, I am not surprised by these findings. They are consistent with the reactions I have experienced.

Most of these women cannot and will not be outspoken about their experience because of the continuing social stigma about abortion. But it's clear many do have strong feelings about the relief they found in the abortion.

CONCERNS ABOUT MASTURBATION

Dear Dr. Menninger:

I was raised in a strict Catholic home in which there was no reference to sex or sexual activity. I had to learn about the facts of life from friends and from books, as well as from my own experience.

There is one area about which I still have uncomfortable feelings. I know some of the magazines and sex-advice books encourage self-pleasure, or masturbation. But I also know that that behavior is forbidden by the church.

For some time, I have been aware that my young son has experienced pleasure from playing with himself, and I am concerned about what to do.

Mrs. A. L.

Concerns about the practice of masturbation or self-pleasure have been expressed for centuries. Back in 1716, a book entitled *Onania, or the Heinous Sin of Self-Pollution* went through eighty editions.

A little over a century ago, Claude Pouillet wrote, "Of all vices and of all the misdeeds which may be properly called crimes against nature which devour humanity, menace its physical vitality and tend to destroy its intellectual and moral faculties, masturbation is one of the greatest and most widespread—no one will deny it."

In those times, an incredible number of diseases were deemed to result from this act—all forms of mental illness, dementia, acne, wasting diseases, etc. Now we know that none results from the act. Yet as recently as 1946, a recognized medical dictionary defined "masturbate" as "to exite the genital organs by unnatural means, to practice self-abuse."

Despite the longstanding and severe admonition against this behavior, Kinsey found that 92 percent of all men and 58 percent of all women admitted to the practice. In Shere Hite's more recent (1976) study of female sexuality, 82 percent of the women reported masturbating.

Though several religious groups have expressed strong positions against this behavior, it can hardly be considered rare, unusual or abnormal. Indeed, it is a common and natural phenomenon which may even play a positive role in the psychosexual development of the child.

That view is espoused in a collection of papers edited by Irwin M. Marcus and John J. Francis ("Masturbation: From Infancy to Senescence"; International Universities Press, New York, 1975). That opinion was also expressed by an overwhelming majority of psychiatrists who responded to a poll in the magazine *Medical Aspects of Human Sexuality.*

Thus, Mrs. L., you should not necessarily push the panic button about the behavior of your son. Unless you feel he is excessively preoccupied with self-pleasure, and his relationships at home and school deteriorate, I would do nothing.

If you continue to be concerned about your son's behavior, I would seek professional counsel. An excessive preoccupation with masturbation is more likely a reflection of other difficulties than a cause of problems in and of itself.

With regard to adult behavior, the survey of psychiatrists found substantial agreement that (1) masturbation by women helps them learn to achieve climax in normal sexual relations, and (2) a majority of married men and women occasionally masturbate.

Although the recent attention given to "self-pleasure" has made it more acceptable and less guilt-laden for many people than in the past, it still is an activity about which people may feel some degree of shame and guilt, and about which they keep their thoughts extremely private.

Internal Stress: Physical Health

THE T.G.I.F. SYNDROME

Many is the time at the end of a strenuous week that I think, "Thank God It's Friday!"—T.G.I.F. I plop down, exhausted, in front of the television set, and I suddenly realize just how much pressure I have been under all week. Of course I'm not alone. Many others have had the same experience.

Several years ago, I realized that some people in that position do not just relax and get it all back together after a strenuous experience. They get sick instead.

Most physicians are keenly aware of the relationship between certain stressful events and the onset of illness. Sometimes the illness develops in the midst of the stress. As in the case of a business executive who, in the midst of very tense and prolonged labor negotiations, had to be hospitalized with a hemorrhaging ulcer.

A number of physicians have studied and rated the stress of life events, correlating the incidence of illness with different kinds of life experiences. They have found the most stressful events are losses of one kind or another—death of a child, spouse, close family member; unfaithfulness of a spouse or divorce; failure in business or being fired.

Often, symptoms develop only after the stressful event is past; it is as if the person does not get sick until it is "safe" to be sick. During the stressful period, the individual rises to the occasion

116

and gives little or no evidence to others that he is under such a severe strain.

But when the pressures are removed, the individual becomes aware of just how much energy and effort were necessary to meet the demands. In addition to a sense of exhaustion, there is the development of additional symptoms or a full-blown illness.

Insofar as the onset of illness parallels the kind of letdown at the end of the work week, I have called the pattern the "T.G.I.F. Syndrome." I've seen it manifested in persons with migraine headaches, who develop them only *after* the acute stress; or canker sores (herpes simplex mouth ulcers) which crop up *after* a stressful experience.

A dramatic illustration of the syndrome was related to me by a World War II Air Force officer. He served uneventfually on his allotted bombing missions and had no problems until the last mission before his scheduled return to the U.S. Even on that mission, he was fine until his plane was back over friendly territory. At that point, he became violently ill to his stomach. The nausea and vomiting persisted and were of such degree that after landing, he required medical attention and was incapacitated for four days.

Some experimental observations have also illustrated the T.G.I.F. phenomenon. One study of "executive" monkeys found that they developed ulcers, but only after the stress tests were over. And a study of the stress on paratroopers in training found one group that didn't show any significant evidence of anxiety until the day after graduation.

The T.G.I.F. Syndrome is more common than many people might realize. And it serves a number of psychological purposes to the person who experiences it. Generally, we are angry about being put under pressure, and the Syndrome can be a way to resolve the anger and resentment felt toward the stress experience. The resentment can't be expressed directly, but by being sick, you escape continuing demands. You also get some attention and sympathy from others, all without having to feel guilty. After all, you can't be blamed for being sick.

Especially significant, however, is the degree to which the T.G.I.F. Syndrome also signals the limits of an individual. In effect, the symptoms let one know that one's ultimate limits of coping are being approached. Indeed, if the limits are not acknowledged, then a recurrence of the illness may be predicted in the face of comparable stress.

HAVE YOU CHECKED YOUR INNER BOILER?

Not long ago, I was visiting with an old high school classmate whom I hadn't seen in a number of years. He was one of the leaders in high school days, and he is now a successful business-man. He was quiet and methodical in the past, apparently easy-going. He still is soft-spoken, but he applies himself to his work with considerable intensity. And he has high blood pressure—hypertension.

It is estimated that twenty-three million Americans have an elevated blood pressure, which makes hypertension a major public health problem in this country. Most people who have hypertension may not realize they do, for it is a silent condition that doesn't usually cause any discomfort in the early stages. My friend discovered his condition during a routine medical check-up.

The problems caused by high blood pressure generally result after a number of years of having the condition. Then there is an increased risk of stroke (hemorrhage into the brain), and other diseases of the heart and circulatory system and kidney failure.

What is your blood pressure? The pressure is the tension level in the closed circulatory system of the body, prompted by the pumping of the heart to force the blood through the body and the elasticity of the blood vessels themselves.

Normally, after the heart has reached the peak of its pumping, the peak blood pressure (known as the systolic blood pressure) is equivalent to a column of mercury 120 to 130 millimeters high. When the heart is between beats, the pressure falls. The low, or diastolic, pressure is normally anywhere from 70 to 90 mm mercury. Thus the normal blood pressure is reported as 120/80 (systolic/diastolic).

Everyone will have variations in blood pressure; when tense or under pressure, it is common for the systolic pressure to rise. It also tends to rise with age, at least in persons living in the industrialized nations. So it may be quite normal for a fifty-year-old to have systolic pressure of 150, with no particular consequences.

The real problem and the diagnosis of hypertension result when the diastolic rises over 100. In other words, the significant elevation in blood pressure is when the whole system is constantly at a higher level, as reflected in the "low" or diastolic reading.

Some groups of people clearly have a greater susceptibility to high blood pressure—people of low socioeconomic status, older women (more than men), and blacks. Indeed, blacks tend to develop hypertension at a younger age and run a more severe course than whites. A black person between the ages of twenty-five and forty-four has approximately fifteen times the chance of a white to die from complications of high blood pressure.

What causes hypertension? For most cases, there is no clear or known cause. Yet it is certain that psychological factors contribute to the problem. Often, the person with high blood pressure tends to be calm and cool, even when faced with an upsetting situation. It is as if he keeps the lid on any expression of anger; the steam in the inner "boiler" is reflected in an increased blood pressure, but not outwardly.

What can be done about it? It can be treated by a medication prescribed by a physician. A Veterans Administration study of over 500 patients followed over a couple of years found treatment of hypertension reduced the incidence of crippling strokes from twelve to one. It also reduced some of the other complications often found with elevated blood pressure.

It is precisely because treatment can make such a difference in the course of a hypertensive's life that you should know if you have the condtion. My friend didn't really like the idea, and he initially was reluctant to admit he had the problem or to take the medication. But he does now; and the odds are he'll live significantly longer because he does.

"I DREAD EVERY DAY . . .
AND EVEN CONSIDERED SUICIDE"

Dear Dr. Menninger:

Seven years ago, I had surgery for cancer. A radical removal of the right parotid gland was necessary. As a result, the right side of my face is paralyzed.

Up until that time, I was an extremely outgoing person. Now I can barely force myself to look at a stranger, because I can't smile and return their friendliness.

I dread every day. At first I even considered suicide. but having a husband and four children, who love me regardless, made me stop thinking like that. Mostly I fear growing older and becoming a very unsatisfied and angry person. I'm thirty-five-years-old and in good health now.

Sincerely,
S. R., California

You have a doubly difficult struggle; not only is your disability obvious but it is the result of cancer. These circumstances evoke various prejudices in others and present you with no small challenge to maintain your emotional composure.

However, you need to ask yourself how much of the reactions are your problem, and how much are really someone else's problem.

Cancer is a self-destructive process where something grows

out of control within us, silently, thereby threatening our existence. Thus it is not surprising that a 1976 Gallup Poll found nearly three out of five (58 percent) Americans feared cancer more than any other disease.

Reactions to your facial appearance may have some childhood origins. Children tend to look first at faces, and also have difficulty understanding why people are different. They may fantasize that if they come in too close contact with someone unusual, they will become like that person.

Though the child grows and learns that such conditions are not contagious, the "child-prejudice" remains. Thus many people avoid others with any condition which appears unsettling or threatening. Sometimes the avoidance is conscious; often people are unaware of this prejudice.

In a study for the Cancer Society, Frances Feldman, professor of social work at the University of Southern California, exposed some of that prejudice. Employers interviewed about work problems and discrimination against ex-cancer patients were amazed such a study was necessary.

They couldn't imagine that over half the ex-cancer patients encountered work problems; nearly a quarter were rejected for jobs because of their cancer treatment. Many experienced strained relationships with coworkers when they returned to work; some coworkers even admitted a fear that the cancer was contagious.

Those are the problems of others. Your problem, Mrs. R., sounds equally to be the result of your own feelings. The Feldman study noted a number of persons recovered from head and neck cancer working in jobs with the most public contact. So you don't have to hide because of your appearance.

It is natural to try and hide your unattractiveness from the world, but few people are without some unattractive feature—appearance, dress, manner—and you must anticipate some hesitance from others.

But significant relationships and true friendships go more than skin deep and result from continued contact which allows the real and lasting beauty to surface in all of the "beasts" in life.

Have faith that the beauty will show to others as it does to your family. Give it a chance to do so. If you can overcome your reluctance to let it show to others, I suspect you will again find the rewarding relationships and experiences you had before your operation.

WHAT CAUSES CANCER?
FLUORIDATION? EMOTIONS?

Dear Dr. Menninger:
Sometimes, it seems like everything we come in contact with may cause cancer. With all the reports about cigarettes and air pollution and food additives causing cancer, it's hard to know what to believe.

Now, I understand some people claim fluoridation of the water to prevent tooth decay also causes cancer. Is this true? And what is the role of emotions in cancer?
Sincerely,
Mrs. M. C.

People keep searching for simple answers to complex problems. This is certainly true in the case of cancer. Some substances have been shown to cause cancer in rats; the proof of causation in humans is not so easy.

Statistical studies are often used in studies of cancer in humans, but they can be misleading. Some reports of a higher incidence of cancer occurring in communities with fluoridated water appear to be a calculated and deliberate misuse of statistics to discredit fluoridation.

Independent investigations by leading medical and scientific organizations in the United States and England, including the National Cancer Institute and the Royal College of Physicians, do not find fluoridation associated with an increase in cancer.

A thorough study of trials throughout the world and reports in scientific literature was made by the World Health Organization. Their conclusion: "The only sign of physiological or pathological change in lifelong users of optimally fluoridated water supplies . . . is that they suffer from less tooth decay."

If you want further information on this subject, an excellent discussion of the cancer scare and fluoridation is in the July 1978 *Consumer Reports* magazine.

With regard to emotions and cancer, the findings are not so clear. Cancer may be thought of as a part of the body that has turned against the self in a destructive way. Similarly, depression is that emotion which has been likened to hate turned inwardly on oneself.

From this perspective, it should not be surprising to discover a frequent association of depression and cancer. In fact, such an association exists. It is hard to determine, however, whether the emotion causes or is caused by the cancer, or whether it is simply associated with it, both being caused by some third factor.

Caroline Bedell Thomas of Johns Hopkins Medical School has been studying graduates of that school, utilizing psychological tests taken when they were in school as well as annual questionnaires about their health. An "unexpected" finding for her was the strong similarity of the psychological profiles of those graduates who developed cancer and those who committed suicide.

A Scottish physician, D. M. Kissen, studied industrial workers and found those who developed cancer had "poor outlets for emotional discharge," and tended to deny or repress their emotions. Other investigators have noted a sense of "hopelessness" and depression in cancer patients.

William Greene, a professor of psychiatry at the University of Rochester, reported in the 1950s that nine out of ten cases of cancer developed at a time when a person felt alone, helpless and hopeless.

While further studies are necessary to clarify the relationship between emotions and cancer, rest assured there is one. Actually, every illness can be influenced by emotional factors—sometimes that influence may be minimal, but often it is greater than most people suspect.

COPING WITH BEING OVERWEIGHT—
SOME DISCOURAGING WORDS

Visiting with a colleague the other day, I was struck by his thin face. "I'm glad you noticed," he said. "I've been reducing since the holidays, and I've lost ten pounds—all by avoiding snacks, baked goods and sweets."

He was obviously pleased with himself. He was feeling better and he hoped to sustain his weight loss.

His motivation is not unique—a good many people recognize they are overweight and would like some easy way to lose that excess. The publicity about the so-called high-protein diet and its complications points to that common concern.

Americans are getting heavier. That much is evident when one compares the weight of Americans examined between 1960 and 1962 with those examined during the years 1971-1974. It is now estimated that from 10 to 30 percent of all Americans weigh almost a third more than their "ideal" weight.

Obesity has become a public health issue, because so many other health problems have been related to it. The increased weight being carried around on the body puts added stress on many of the body systems, particularly the heart and circulatory system, and the bones and joints.

Obese people are more prone to develop gall bladder disease, strokes, diabetes, heart disease and hypertension (high blood pressure). Obese women have been noted to have more menstrual disorders and more cancer of the uterus (endometrial cancer).

In the face of the extent of excess weight and the widespread concern about obesity, it is a bit distressing to find many investigators confessing ignorance about what causes obesity and how best to treat it. Yet that was the conclusion of an international group of researchers who met in a 1977 conference on Obesity and the American Public, sponsored by the National Institutes of Health.

Science magazine reporter Gina Bari Kolata reported on that conference, and she noted the researchers' observations that "discouragingly few people lose weight with any drug, diet, or other treatment; and even those who do lose weight are likely to regain it later."

The conference participants also acknowledged that many of the theories about obesity don't hold up to careful study. Many widely held beliefs about the causes and effects of obesity are either not firmly established or are just not true.

Some studies now show that social factors are as important, or more so, in causing obesity than genetic or metabolic factors. As with many other aspects of human behavior, a most important influencing factor in the obesity of children is their parents.

Fat parents tend to have fat children. So notes Stanley Garn of the Center for Human Growth and Development in Ann Arbor, Michigan. This holds true whether the children are direct offspring of the parents or adopted. By age seventeen, children of obese parents will be three times as fat as children of lean parents. (Their pets are also fatter.)

According to the researchers, only a minority—between 5 and 20 percent—of obese people can lose weight and then keep it off after dieting. And no one diet has been consistently found to be any better over the long haul than any other.

Some of the more radical treatments for severe obesity, like the surgical intestinal bypass operation, may have a higher success rate, but the expense and risk are considerable. On occasion, the treatment may turn out to be worse than the disease itself.

The suggestion of the conference researchers is that the greatest hope for combatting obesity will be in better education about health and nutrition, and that education should include specific information about the size of "normal" portions of food.

In addition to helping people with their intake of food, effective treatment of obesity must include exercise—helping the individual burn up more of his food by regular physical activity.

AFTER A HYSTERECTOMY—
ARE YOU ANY LESS A WOMAN?

Dear Dr. Menninger:

Would you do an article on the effects of a complete hysterectomy?

What does it do regarding the sex life and emotions? Are there any aftereffects and how should a couple handle it? Other than having the baby-producing equipment removed, does it make a woman any less a woman?

I've been told I need one, but am wondering how it will affect me, my husband and our marriage. Is this similar to a vasectomy in a man? I know it's more serious. How does a vasectomy affect a man's emotions, when he can no longer produce children?

Thank you for any help you can give me and others like me.

Sincerely,
Mrs. M. G.

You raise questions commonly presented by women facing the possibility of a hysterectomy. As you presumably know, the term refers to the surgical removal of the uterus (womb), an operation which (it is estimated) 25 percent of women over fifty have had. And the procedure is being performed more often on younger women.

Sometimes there is confusion about what is included in the operation. Literally, the hysterectomy—partial or complete—refers just to the uterus. When the ovaries and tubes are also removed, the proper term is a pan-hystero-salpingo-oophorectomy.

What are the aftereffects? The results depend, in large part, on your feelings about yourself and the circumstances which prompt the surgery.

For instance, if the reason for the hysterectomy is evidence of early cancer, or excessive uterine bleeding which does not respond to hormonal treatment, or a precancerous condition, the surgery can provide relief.

The one definite result, as you note, is the loss of ability to have babies. If you see yourself as having value only as a producer of children, the loss of the uterus may be experienced as a profound devaluation. But the uterus is not the organ which makes you feminine, and there is no reason to assume your femininitiy or womanhood should be at all changed.

Other emotional reactions vary. Generally, women who have been active in several areas in life handle the surgery better than women whose life has been totally devoted to being a mother and homemaker.

What about your sex life? If it has been satisfactory before the procedure, there is no reason to assume it will be otherwise afterward. The operation does not change that part of your anatomy which is necessary for normal, satisfactory sexual relations and climax.

Indeed, becaue of the freedom from fear of pregnancy, some women experience a hysterectomy as sexually liberating.

In any case, the procedure should not present any untoward problems for you, your husband, or your marriage. If you or your husband do have concerns, it is best to discuss them together and get them out in the open.

A hysterectomy is a major surgical procedure and thus should not be taken lightly. As with any major surgery, there is the potential for complications and death. If you have doubts about having the operation, you should feel free to get a second medical consultation before having it done.

The vasectomy, in contrast, is a minor surgical procedure which can be performed in a doctor's office. The man's reactions, as with the woman's for her surgery, will depend, in part, on his feelings toward himself and the circumstances which prompt the procedure.

Internal Stress: Mental Health

"CUCKOO'S NEST"—WHO'S CUCKOO?

Who's really crazy in this world? The folks who are sent to the mental hospitals? Or maybe the people who work there? Recently I went to see the movie version of Ken Kesey's *One Flew Over the Cuckoo's Nest,* and that movie raises these same questions.

I had a particular interest in seeing this film, since a year ago I played a small part in a community theater production of *Cuckoo's Nest* which subsequently won first prize in a state community theater competition. Of course, as a clinical director in a public mental hospital, I also wanted to see how the film production handled the psychiatric hospital scenes.

As one who had acted in the stage version of the show, I found the movie missing some of the elements which added power to the drama on stage. Much less obvious in the movie, for instance, was the powerful struggle between the "Big Nurse" Ratched and R. P. McMurphy for control of the ward.

The author is clearly critical of psychiatry, so in the story the quality of the psychiatrists and psychiatric treatment is less than adequate. I suspect therefore that the average movie-goer will not realize that the image of state hospital treatment in the movie is not the way it is in many settings today.

McMurphy (played by Jack Nicholson) is a so-called psychopath who fakes being mentally ill in order to get transferred out of the work farm. He looks for an easier time at the mental hospital where he is sent for an evaluation.

In the hospital, McMurphy is assigned to a ward which is tightly controlled by Nurse Ratched. While she runs it as a pseudodemocracy, she is really calling all the shots, controlling ward privileges, music, television, etc. Of course, this is all done in the "best interests" of all the patients.

The manner by which the nurse maintains her control is not immediately apparent in the movie, but is clearly evident in the play. The psychiatrist is rather ineffectual and leaves the treatment up to the nurse. Those who get out of control are referred to the disturbed ward for electroshock treatment (ECT) or ultimately for psychosurgery.

How much does this mirror the current psychiatric scene? Little, if at all. Regrettably there still are many public mental hospitals in older buildings with open wards and tub rooms, unable to meet the standards of the Joint Commission on the Accreditation of Hospitals.

In the Topeka (KS) State Hospital, which I know best and which is JCAH accredited, the patients are all housed in modern, one-story buildings, with nearly all one or two bedrooms. The facilities are much like a modern college dormitory. Electroshock treatment is rarely practiced and psychosurgery not at all.

ECT is a subject which can provoke much emotion and sometimes irrational reactions, as in the legislation passed in California in late 1974 which severely restricts its use. That law is an unfortunate example of legislators telling doctors how to practice medicine without understanding what they are doing.

Modern ECT is not portrayed in the movie, either in application or technique. ECT can be life-saving for some depressed and suicidal patients; it is of no benefit and is improperly administered to behavior disorders of the nature suggested by McMurphy. And patients who receive ECT today are first given a short-acting general anesthetic and a muscle relaxant to limit the intensity of the electrically induced convulsion.

As a portrayal of a provocative power struggle and as a commentary on mental hospitals twenty-five years ago, *Cuckoo's Nest* is good drama. It should not be taken to represent current psychiatric practice in most state hospitals, including the Oregon facility where it was filmed.

"IT'S TIME TO BRING CONCERNS
TO THE PEOPLE"

Dear Dr. Menninger:

I was delighted to read about your father's work in mental health awareness. That has become a growing concern in my own life. In fact, I walked out of a graduate university scholarship to work in mental health services.

At any rate, could you let me know specifically what it was your father did? Would you have any of his speeches or any of the highlights of his career in terms of directly influencing legislatures?

Also, do you have any idea what is going on right now in the way of public education for everyone on mental health and mental health services?

So May was Mental Health Month! I didn't know. I would have personally designed and posted announcements for transit buses everywhere if I had been more aware.

I believe it's time that people begin to associate mental health with maybe several martinis for lunch rather than Charles Manson tendencies. It's time to bring concerns to the people as both financiers and consumers of mental health services.

I would like to know where to begin, I guess.
Thank you.
K. B.
Cleveland, Ohio

Interest in what is going on right now in mental health is also evident in the White House, since President Carter appointed a National Commission on Mental Health and named his wife Rosalynn to head it.

Mental illness is still much misunderstood and often frightening to people. Many are so unsettled by the subject that they stay as far away from it as they can. Thus, public education is very much needed in this field.

At times over the years, the media have played an important role in education about mental illness and the care provided by public mental health facilities. Some television shows have been sensitive and constructive in their approach to the topic.

This is not always true, as evidenced by a recent ABC television show, which was particularly unfortunate. In an atmosphere of anger and condemnation, that show portrayed what might best be labeled half-truths. It pictured some of the worst treatment for mental illness, without keeping it in full perspective.

In years past, the care of the mentally ill in most state hospitals has left much to be desired. In many states, that care still falls short of the ideal. And you can find places where it is really bad. But to imply that treatment in *all* public mental hospitals is harmful, inhuman and barbaric is unconscionable!

It is true that budgets for mental health care in most states are nowhere near what might be preferred. Most state hospitals spend less than half of the daily fee of $125-per-patient charged in

138

one first-class private psychiatric hospital. And mental health care is no different from any other service. You get what you pay for.

It was to emphasize the importance of adequate money for care of the mentally ill that my father, Dr. William C. Menninger, spoke to so many legislatures. (His remarks have been published in a book of his collected papers entitled *A Psychiatrist for a Troubled World,* published in 1967 after he died. It is unfortunately now out of print.)

His remarks did prompt legislators to respond. In Ohio, they increased the tax on alcoholic beverages to raise more money for mental hospitals. In Kentucky, after he spoke in 1956, the appropriations were increased by over a million dollars. In California, a year later, they gave mental health an additional three million dollars and passed supportive legislation for community mental health services.

Programs of public education are largely dependent upon local or state initiative. You can help by working through your local mental health association, and I suggest you start there. If you cannot locate a local or state group, contact the National Association for Mental Health, 1800 North Kent St., Arlington, Virginia 22209.

DEPRESSION—REAL, NOT IMAGINARY

Dear Dr. Menninger:

Depression and anxiety.

There have been several articles on this subject in the news media but no real explanation for it.

Mine all started when I had an operation two years ago, then I had a breakdown—sleeplessness, nerves, crying, loss of weight, all of it. Thank goodness I recovered from most of that. But I still have to take a mild tranquilizer to keep going.

One would think I have nothing to worry about—a wonderful husband, five beautiful children and nine darling grandchildren. Yet, I still have the terrible exhaustion and at times a nervous feeling inside like I'm going to explode.

How do you make people understand when I look fine and am only in my early sixties? I get so disgusted with myself when I feel this way and can't keep going like I want to. I try not to show it or worry my family, but I'm thoroughly sick of trying to explain it to anyone.

I'm so thankful I am not physically ill. I went through menopause with flying colors, worked for fifteen years, am now retired with my husband and we have a comfortable income. So why? Why?

I know so many people read your column, so if you can somehow help the ordinary class of people who have not experienced this to understand it is a real thing and not imaginary. You can't just be rid of it by wishful thinking.

Sincerely,

Mrs. I. M.

I'm delighted to share your story to remind people how common and real depression is, even when it may not be obvious to others.

The emotional reaction of depression is evidenced by being down and discouraged, dragging, without much appetite, having trouble sleeping, etc., and it can occur in mild and severe forms. No one is immune; it can happen to anybody.

Depression in part reflects anger which is turned on to oneself, because it can't be expressed outwardly. Thus, some people are more vulnerable because of the way they handle their resentment and anger. There is also some evidence that some people are more vulnerable to depression because of some biochemical characteristics, although this is still being researched.

As a general rule, depression follows some kind of loss, which may be real or imaginary. The loss may be a friend, loved one, a job, a valued possession. The loss may be more psychological— a sense of security, a loss of youth, a loss of a familiar role in life.

Sometimes the loss is obvious to others; sometimes it is not. There are even occasions where people feel like they've lost something when on the surface it appears they've gained something, as in the case of a new mother becoming depressed after giving birth to a child.

As one grows older, there can be other losses. Particularly important may be the loss of a meaningful, contributing role in life. It can be devastating to feel unnecessary in life; we all need to be needed.

One study of older people carried out at Duke University found that just by being a subject in the study gave participants a new sense of meaning in life. It increased their longevity as compared to a control group of older people.

Sometimes you may hold off a depression until something overwhelms you—like the operation you cited. Then some little losses may all add up and lead to the reaction.

It is well to recognize that's what's happening and accept it as a real struggle, however imaginary it may seem to others. The symptoms may seem to be physical, and it can seem frustrating when the doctor checks you out and finds you physically okay.

The best answer is not to seek the sympathy of family and friends. Deal with it matter-of-factly; let them know you have limits. Meanwhile, make a renewed effort to find new compensations for your losses. And utilize medication when you find it helpful—as prescribed by your doctor.

PARANOIA—WHEN WE NEED
TO BLAME OTHERS

Dear Dr. Menninger:
Does anyone ever recover from paranoia? I have been under psychiatric care since 1964 and have had three acute attacks. I was hospitalized for four months in 1964 and three weeks each 1971 and 1974.

During the last episode, I had complete amnesia for a week. I could remember nothing of that week except for two events, the memory of which was triggered by gazing at something and touching it.

The psychiatrist told me not to remember—let sleeping dogs lie, so to speak. But I have heard vis-a-vis the grapevine that I have been diagnosed as paranoid.

Would it be feasible for you to do a column on this subject? How many kinds of paranoia are there? Are any recoverable? What is the accepted form of treatment? Does age have anything to do with recovery or onset of the disease? (I was forty-four at the time of my first attack.) What about paranoia coupled with old age?

Thank you.
Miss M. G.
California

Most people are reluctant to accept the responsibility for why

143

they are the way they are, and they like to blame others for their problems. We all do that at times, in order to maintain our self-esteem and sense of personal integrity.

The paranoid condition is the extreme state where blaming others is the total explanation for what's happening to you and where the blame is not founded in reality.

It results from the use of a mental mechanism labeled projection. If you are beset by feelings or thoughts which are unacceptable to you and which threaten to overwhelm you, you may protect your psychological integrity by projecting those thoughts and feelings onto others.

As a means for coping with unacceptable inner thoughts and feelings, the paranoid process may be seen in a wide range of emotional states.

Often the condition begins with a sense that other people are paying excessive attention to you or talking about you. You believe the glances and actions of others all have some specific reference to you. You may feel they are saying bad things and wish to harm you.

The condition may progress to a dominant sense of being persecuted. You become preoccupied with protecting yourself against that persecution; but you are rarely successful, since the persecution is actually a construction in your own mind from which you cannot escape.

For some people, this pattern of coping is used to an extensive degree throughout life and is quite fixed in their thinking and behavior.

Others manifest the pattern in response to a stressful period of life—young adulthood, the midlife or change-of-life period, and old age. In some, there is associated with it a serious disorder in thinking.

The prognosis varies according to when it develops and the seriousness of the thinking disorder associated with it. When the onset is in the midlife period, the prognosis is reasonably good.

The treatment depends upon the overall emotional state. Psychiatric hospitalization may be necessary at times to provide a nonthreatening and supportive environment. Sometimes tranquillizer medication is helpful, sometimes psychotherapy. In some instances, in acute cases, electroshock treatment is beneficial.

In all instances, treatment may be resisted because you are so deeply convinced that the problems are outside you. Thus you do not believe you need to change yourself or that you should be subject to any treatment.

Another cause of your paranoia may be fears that are a reaction to some unacceptable thoughts deep within your mind of which you are not consciously aware. Of course, everybody has had frightening conscious thoughts; they are common in childhood and throughout life.

But sometimes in the deep recesses of the mind, there are thoughts and wishes which we can't consciously face. Usually these thoughts are tied in some way to unacceptable feelings of love or hate. Whatever be the precise wish or thought, it becomes a "thought crime" to be kept under wraps.

The thought crime may simply be buried in the mind, filed away in a Fibber McGee-like closet of thoughts and feelings we don't like to face. Or it may be turned around and laid onto someone else. Thus the thought surfaces, but as what someone else is thinking about you, rather than what you think of yourself.

In this way, your mind plays a trick on you, leading you to believe that the criticism you feel is from others. Instead of being "convicted" yourself, it is others who say it about you; and you can be angry at them. That's much easier than being angry with yourself.

The mental process of attributing to others feelings that really originate within your own mind is called "projection." One of the clues which suggests the presence of projection is the difference between your perception and your wife's. It is confirmed by your hearing things which you cannot rationally explain, like hearing people talking about you even with the car windows closed. Those voices are coming from within your own mind.

It is hard to constantly criticize yourself with doubts. Some people do and they are depressed—depression is anger turned in on oneself. Projection protects you from becoming depressed, because you are angry at others. But your constant worry keeps you unable to function at your best.

When fears become so troubling that they interfere with your life, you need some help. Start by talking with someone you can trust, your family doctor or clergyman. If they can't help you put your thoughts in perspective—then seek help from a mental health professional. He or she should also help you work out the problems of the job and retirement.

IS ALCOHOLISM AN ILLNESS?

Do you think alcoholism is an illness?

That question was posed to me in a question-and-answer period following a recent public address. The woman who put the question to me thought more and more people considered excessive drinking as some kind of misbehavior rather than an illness.

Certainly it can be an illness, and it can also mask other serious emotional problems. But the line between normal drinking and excessive dependency upon alcohol (alcoholism) is not easy to draw. After all, during any given month, one survey noted, 58 percent of the population drink alcoholic beverages—that's about 125 million Americans.

Of those current drinkers, 62 percent report having one or two drinks on an average day; 22 percent have three or four drinks a day. Fourteen percent, or roughly seventeen million Americans, admit to having five or more drinks on an average day!

Excessive use of alcohol is a significant problem in this country. The substance is widely available, relatively cheap, and has the capacity to dull your judgment as you take more and more of it. It works like an emotional anesthetic, deadening anxiety and emotional pain.

The capacity of alcohol to reduce one's inhibitions makes it particularly effective as a "social lubricant" at cocktail parties.

But this same quality is involved in the problems associated with alcohol—it continues to be the drug most associated with crime, violence, auto accidents, marital problems and child abuse.

What makes alcohol abuse particularly difficult to deal with is the tendency of many people to deny their dependency upon it. People can get "hooked" on alcohol and be unable to see the degree to which it controls them, instead of vice versa. That is part of the "illness" of alcoholism.

The alcohol-dependent person is most reluctant to give it up, feeling great discomfort without it. He or she may strongly object to any accusation that the drinking is a problem. Thus the partner in a marriage can feel helpless about confronting the spouse with the criticism or suspicion of excessive drinking.

There is no painless way to cope with alcoholism. But there is an increasing number of good programs, many which have developed with the support of recovered alcoholics, to help people come to grips with the problem.

How can you tell if someone is an alcoholic? There are a number of checklists available, but a recent study of the department of psychiatry at the Washington University School of Medicine in St. Louis found three questions would pretty well screen alcoholics:

Has your family ever objected to your drinking?

Did you ever think you drank too much in general?

Have others ever said you drink too much for your own good?

These screening questions aren't foolproof, but nearly all (96 percent) of the definite and probable alcoholics were identified by a "yes" answer to them. What about you?

DOES HOSPITALIZATION HELP
CURE MENTAL ILLNESS?

Dear Dr. Menninger:

Our family has gone through great anguish recently because of my mother. Over the past few years, she has become increasingly difficult in her behavior. Now she is excessively fearful. She keeps the window blinds pulled and the doors locked and double-bolted. She is sure that people are watching her and going to harm her.

Recently she was pestering the police department with phone calls about a car supposedly driving by her house repeatedly. They could not find anything unusual, but she is sure the Mafia or the Communists or someone is out to get her. And she is not taking care of herself or the house.

Our doctor suggested that she go to the mental hospital, but she does not want to go. I've heard a lot of bad things about mental hospitals, and I honestly don't know whether to encourage her to go or not. Sometimes I read of the lack of staff at the state hospital, and I don't know what's best for her. What would you suggest?

Sincerely,
Mrs. R. Q.

The current estimate is that approximately one in every ten persons in this country will be hospitalized at some time or another during his or her life for emotional problems. Yet there are some who argue that no one should ever be hospitalized for mental illness and that hospitals make patients worse.

I don't agree. I work in a psychiatric hospital and I have seen the help it can provide.

What kind of help? Often, the most important is that it provides a different, protected environment for an anxious and fearful person. The hospital becomes a haven from life's stormy seas. Your mother would quite likely find some relief and a feeling of protection once in a hospital setting.

In the hospital, with twenty-four-hour professional observation, a more thorough and careful evaluation of the emotional illness is possible. The contact with the therapeutic personnel can be valuable in spotting special problems and helping your mother work them through, as well as to observe the effect of any prescribed medication.

One aspect of hospitalization which is not always fully exploited is the degree to which patients can help other patients. This interaction can be extremely beneficial, both directly and as part of the therapeutic activities.

It is sometimes painful to realize that relatives can be part of the problem, but one other aspect of hospitalization may be some limitation on the visits and calls from relatives or friends.

Finally, a hospital offers a place where one can safely let down or "regress," retreating from everyday responsibilities. A patient can be looked after and fed, psychologically as well as physically. Being allowed to function in a less mature and less independent manner provides time for emotional "healing" and restoration.

In the past, with the exception of some expensive private psychiatric hospitals, the only facilities available were the public mental hospitals which were largely the responsibility of state government. In only a few states have they been funded to provide the best possible care. Even in the state hospital where I work, one of the best funded in the country, the expenditure per patient per day is less than half what it costs in the private sector.

In many locations there are now psychiatric units in general hospitals, which have made brief hospitalization for emotional problems easier and more acceptable. But there will continue to be a need for some mental hospitals for the more difficult and less responsive emotional illnesses.

Therefore, I would urge you to find out what kind of facilities you do have in your community for the hospital care of the emotionally ill. If the community mental health center facilities or the public mental hospitals are not adequate, join your local mental health association and work to improve those facilities.

SELF-HELP FOR THE MENTALLY ILL

Last fall, I wrote of a visit with a group of former mental patients who were helping each other get it together, meeting weekly under the auspices of the local mental health association. On that occasion, the group, known as "Breakthrough," was sharing ideas about overcoming the stigma of their condition and getting a job after a bout of mental illness.

Life is not easy for persons whose emotional problems get in the way of everyday life adjustment. A wide range of mental health professionals and clinics provide services to these troubled people. And there are also some significant self-help organizations in this field. Two of the better known such organizations trace their origins to Alcoholics Anonymous—Recovery, Inc. and Emotional Health Anonymous.

In 1937, just two years after the founding of AA, Recovery, Inc., was originated by the late Dr. Abraham Low, a Chicago psychiatrist and neurologist. In the thirty-nine years since, Recovery has spread throughout the United States, Canada and Puerto Rico, with more than one thousand active groups and roughly fifteen thousand members. Its headquarters remain in Chicago.

The Recovery Method, as it is called, is based on the original principles outlined by Dr. Low in *Mental Health Through Will Training,* which is used as a text for panel discussion.

A retired free-lance writer in Cleveland shared with me a schedule of twenty-nine Recovery groups meeting weekly in that metropolitan area, and he observed that the "organization is a haven of refuge and relief for hundreds of Clevelanders afflicted with the problems of nervous symptoms, including former mental patients and also those who are afflicted with the stress of daily living in one context or another." As succinctly stated by a woman who is a Recovery group leader in western Kansas, "Members are trained to accept responsibility for their own mental health and foster self-leadership."

A survey conducted for Recovery found that 70 percent of the members have received some treatment for their problems, but only half (52 percent) have been hospitalized for emotional illness. The organization does expect "each member who needs professional care to follow the authority of and to cooperate with his personal physician and/or other professionals at all times. Recovery does not offer advice, counseling, diagnosis or treatment; it provides self-help aftercare only."

A key to self-help is nonprofessional leadership. Indeed, while mental health professionals are welcome to attend Recovery meetings and participate as members, they are quite specifically denied leadership roles.

Emotional Health Anonymous is a California-based organization of recent vintage. Its program for the mentally ill is quite literally parallel to the program of Alcoholics Anonymous, with Twelve Steps, Twelve Traditions and "Just for Today." It is headquartered in the Los Angeles area (EHA, 2420 San Gabriel Blvd., Rosemead, California 91770).

It identifies itself as a fellowship program "to help you recover from emotional or mental illness." The informational brochure about the program acknowledges its debt to AA for permission

153

to adapt the AA recovery program to fit the emotionally ill instead of the alcoholic.

EHA defines emotionally ill persons as "individuals whose emotions interfere with their daily living in any way whatsoever, or to any degree, as recognized by themselves." And the first Step is "we admitted we were powerless over our emotions— that our lives had become unmanageable."

A member of an EHA group in Long Beach, California, wrote enthusiastically that "I am a new creation since I worked these twelve steps for my emotional problems." And as with Recovery, Inc., there is a commitment to "remain forever non-professional."

As a mental health professional, I heartily salute the efforts of these organizations Dr. Low started Recovery because he was keenly aware that there were many more people in need of help than professionals to provide that help. These organizations have been and will certainly continue supplementing and complementing services available from mental health professionals.

Internal Stress: Being Different

CAN WE ELIMINATE PREJUDICE?

After a presidential primary election, a political pundit observed that prejudice is alive and well and as potent as ever in determining people's choices at the ballot box.

That reminded me of a visit with a high-level government official some years back. Discussing some of the problems of the large cities, he asked me, "How can we eliminate prejudice?"

Presumably he thought because I am a psychiatrist, I had some magic answer to this question. (That's a mistaken assumption many people have.) My answer was simple and straightforward and not what he expected: We aren't going to eliminate prejudice! Because the causes of prejudice lie too deep in the human personality.

Webster defines prejudice as a preconceived judgment or opinion, an opinion without just grounds or before sufficient knowledge, an unreasonable inclination or objection. While the term usually refers to feeling against someone or something, it can be positive as well as negative. We can be prejudiced toward certain foods or clothes or politics just as much as we may be prejudiced against some people.

Our prejudices are a function of emotions—the eternal, complicating factors in life. They originate in early childhood from feelings we have about things we don't or can't understand. Indeed, as Webster notes, the roots of prejudice lie in feelings "before sufficient knowledge."

As adults, we may like to believe that all men and women are created equal. But it doesn't take the child long to realize it's really otherwise. There are real differences, and there are many imagined differences above and beyond the real differences. And many feelings are prompted by both the real and imagined differences.

One set of feelings comes from realizing that there are "haves" and "have-nots." The "haves," as they realize they have something others do not, fear the loss of what they have and try to protect themselves. The "have-nots," as they become aware of what they lack, resent the status of being without and strive to make up or compensate for their deficiency.

Being a "have" or a "have-not" relates to many conditions— sex, race, socioeconomic status. There is even the basic "have-not" status which every child experiences, living in the land of giants, being relatively helpless, not completely sure he will grow up to become a giant himself.

As children move out of the home into school, they become increasingly aware of differences and struggle to explain them. The basic difficulty is that a young child doesn't have the knowledge to explain the differences or understand them. But he feels them. Unable to justify the feelings in rational adult terms, he comes up with other formulations.

He may deny that differences really exist and rely on childish fantasies of magical power or hope that all will turn out equal in the end, when he is grown up (if that ever really happens). Or he may displace feelings of inadequacy onto someone else who has "less," or who is felt to be less adequate; he thus elevates his self-esteem by putting someone else down.

Yet another complicating factor has been cited by the late Dr.

Lawrence Kubie, a Baltimore psychoanalyst. The child has mixed feelings about his own body—on the one hand, he has a secret, guilty pride in it; on the other hand, he has hidden feelings of shame. And it is hard to come to grips with both good and bad in oneself. The psychological solution is to bury the inner "bad" feelings, deny their existence within, and instead to lay them onto others, putting all the "badness" outside.

How can we eliminate prejudice? We can't, any more than we can eliminate all disease or maladjustment. It is part of the human condition. We can attempt to understand our prejudices and to admit the biases we have, but we can't eliminate them.

THE SOLO WOMAN IN A MAN'S
WORLD—AN ISOLATE

With issues like the Equal Rights Amendment and the Affirma-
tive Action Program struggling for attention, the rights of wom-
en is a subject of much discussion these days.

Yet, male dominance in our society is pretty definite wherever
you look—in business, government, on television, etc.

Most men—even those men who support the women's movement—don't realize the degree to which they "put down" wom-
en, often quite subconsciously. Notice at a party how men dominate conversation in a mixed group, often refusing to acknowledge the comments of a woman.

A fourth-year woman medical student recounted to me experiences while working with her classmates. Consistently, they
assumed she didn't have much to say; if she did, they tended to
tune her out. She simply wasn't accorded much value.

At the University of Pennsylvania, Psychiatrist Carol Wolman and Group Behavior Specialist Hal Frank looked at male-
female interaction in another context. They studied the behavior
of men in groups with lone woman members.

Even though the solo woman in the group had academic or
professional credentials which were equal to the men in the
group, she was consistently denied a role of equality in the
group.

When group members started to interact, the woman was not

158

allowed to compete freely for status. She was placed in a deviant or isolated role, which generally made her unhappy.

If she did try to compete openly, the men often simply ignored her assertive behavior. Or else they labeled her as being "bitchy" or a manipulator. They seemed to be more threatened by competition from her than from other men.

The more a woman became identified as expressing feelings, which was sometimes one of the tasks of the group, the more the men became intellectual. Indeed, the presence of the lone woman prompted the men to become hypermasculine in some ways, adhering to the male stereotype.

Wollman and Frank postulate that in the all-male group, there is normally a "hunting-group" atmosphere. When a woman enters the group, the men have to give up that atmosphere and they resent it. But they can't express their hostility directly toward the woman.

Further, there are other subtle fears of the men. One is that the woman will act as a weak person and demand that the men take care of her, violating the expectation that group members be independent and tough.

Or they fear that the woman will compete successfully with them and embarrass them by her competence, thereby threatening their masculinity.

Finally, there is a fear that she will stir up sexual rivalry among men in the group, disrupting their friendships and violating the expectation that sexual feelings are taboo.

Wolman and Frank observed that either the woman could accept the position of being an isolate in the group, or she could accept the "low" status at the bottom of the pecking order in the group, minimizing competition while letting other group members get to know her as a person.

159

If a woman finds herself in an excluded role and feels unhappy about it, she should realize that powerful group forces operate to keep her there. She should not blame herself for being inadequate or become depressed. Rather, she should mobilize emotional support from outside the group if she needs it.

Most significantly, Wolman and Frank advise administrators in businesses and organizations to avoid setting up groups with lone women members. Rather, groups should include two or three women if they are to have any.

PROBLEMS OF SINGLES—AN ANSWER IN MIAMI

In many large cities, there is an increasing number of isolated and lonely people—"singles"—who would like to find companionship. But they don't know where to turn.

Sometimes the option of living alone is by voluntary choice. Sometimes it's the result of fate. Sometimes it's because the person has not been able to find a compatible partner.

In Miami, Nancy Webb Hatton is a single. She is a dynamic, ambitious young journalist who separated from her husband this past year and moved south to become a reporter for the *Miami Herald.*

She got interested in some of the issues facing others like herself, and she responded by developing a regular weekly column for the *Herald* on the problems of singles.

Some of her columns discuss single individuals in different life situations: a twenty-six-year-old barmaid who is divorced and raising a daughter and who wonders just how well she will survive while "making enough to exist but not to get ahead."

A single, graying, free and thirty-six-year-old former librarian who enjoys her "freedom." When she realized that she "wouldn't be able to retire until 2005, working for the government," she took her retirement fund, moved to Miami, and invested in a handicrafts shop.

A thirty-four-year-old single father who is frustrated in his search for a wife "because of the demands of work and fatherhood."

Ms. Hatton has written about specific situations affecting single people—"They See Red Over Income Tax." "When Cooking for Yourself, Say: 'I'm Worth Cooking For.'" "Traveling Alone, Hotel and Travel Rates Are Higher." And she's researched some tips for singles in cooking, traveling, and taxes.

Yet the most impressive reaction came when she shared a letter from a young man who wrote:

"If you randomly interview fifty single girls, you will certainly find that thirty of them will swear that they want nothing more than the normal family life replete with loving husband and shaggy dog.

"They will, also, without taking a breath, tell you something like, 'But, I just can't find anyone decent!'"

The letter writer proceeded to recount his and his friends' encounters with single women, all of whom presented some drawback—wanting to borrow money, being geared to a $50,000-a-year lifestyle, feeling a repulsion for any sexual contact, etc.

He continued, "Lest you wonder, all of this has not left me bitter. Not at all. But I have come to the conclusion that many divorcees/single girls are paying lip service when they desire a home and family."

He wondered where to find a decent person. More than one hundred "decent" women and men called the paper or wrote in response to Ms. Hatton's column, and the paper devoted several columns to their responses. Here are a couple:

"I understand and feel sorry for him. However, he is mistaken. There are still decent women around. I am using the term loosely, because decent women do not 'go around.' They are usually met through friends or organizations . . .

"Please give him the advice my sister always gives me—'You must kiss many frogs before you meet your prince (princess)!'... I've often wondered as I trembled at a singles bar whether the guys were facing the same fears and questions. Now I know for sure that they are."

It's apparent that there are a lot of singles in Miami looking for assistance. And the example set by the *Herald* and Ms. Hatton in spotlighting those problems is a good one to follow, for the singles' problems aren't limited to Miami.

"A LIFE THAT WAS RIGHT FOR ME"

Dear Dr. Menninger:

I am a Catholic, and I thank you for your calm, factual discussion of masturbation. I have lived as a Lesbian since 1932. In all those years, I have lived with only two women. I lost my last partner this spring after almost thirty-three years. She was also Catholic.

Perhaps God will punish me, I do not know; but I cannot believe he will. I do not believe that Christ at any time proclaimed that homosexuality was a sin.

My conscience does not bother me; I go to church regularly and take communion. I have been a convert for almost thirty-three years. I recall the history courses in high school which told of the papacy being bought and sold. Yet, in my heart, I feel Catholicism is the original Christian church, and I have always been deeply attracted to it.

I am as I am. I am not advising that each one go out and try homosexuality, or masturbation, or group sex, or whatever. I just believe it is right for me. I'm not advocating it.

In college, I went with men and had sexual relations with some of them. When I attended, in 1928, not all the women were as "proper" as it is assumed we were. However, I never found satisfaction until my first experiences with my first woman friend. She divorced her husband, her

164

second marriage, and we lived together happily, with her child, for over ten years.

I find it difficult to have complete faith in a pope who in all his years and with all his knowledge cannot or will not admit that this is a changing world.

At my age, I cannot get too uptight over the proclamations. I figure life will go on, and we "half-Catholics," as I assume we are, will go on attending church, praying and hoping for some better understanding at some time in the future. In many ways, it seems time has been frozen for the church.

Actually, I don't feel a bit like a criminal, nor do I feel "sick." I have lived a life that for me was right. I cannot concern myself with man-made statements, regardless of who the man is.

Sincerely,
D. S.

Thank you for sharing your experience and thoughts about what continues to be a much misunderstood and maligned situation. Not long after getting your letter, I received a book in which you would be interested. It is a thoughtful discussion of this whole subject by a Jesuit priest, John J. McNeill, entitled *The Church and the Homosexual* (Sheed Andrews and McMeel, Kansas City).

Father McNeill first started his writing in 1970, and the publication of his view was delayed for several years, pending the approval of his superiors in the religious order. The book reviews the major thoughts which have traditionally dominated the thinking of Catholic theologians concerning homosexuality.

He points out how many of these views are open to serious

question today. For instance, in contrast to the traditional view, McNeill argues that the homosexual condition is according to the will of God, not contrary to it. "Always and everywhere a certain percentage of humans emerge . . . as predominately homosexuality oriented through no fault of their own."

He goes on to suggest that "God had a divine purpose in so creating human nature that a certain percentage of human beings are homosexual. Rather than being a menace to the community in general and the family in particular, they have an important role to play in preserving and strengthening values . . ."

Finally, he believes in the possibility of morally good homosexual relationships in which the love of the partners may bring them closer to God, rather than alienate them from God. His views are indeed challenging.

WHO IS SPEAKING OUT TO COUNTER
ANTI-HOMOSEXUAL MOVEMENT?

Dear Dr. Menninger:
I'm surprised that no one in the psychiatric profession has stuck his neck out to counter all the anti-homosexual feeling now prevalent.

Correct me if I'm wrong, but it was my impression the American Psychiatric Association characterized homosexuality as being a maladaptation—such as being left-handed. This was four years ago. Has there been any change?

Surely there must be some homosexuals whom we find objectionable, but can't the same be said for heterosexuals?

I'm surprised that no member of your association has come forth with a simple clarifying statement.

In other words, who says homosexuality is an illness or immorality?

Sincerely,
M. R.

It would be nice if a simple clarifying statement would quell some of the intense fervor surrounding homosexuality. But I suspect that is only wishful thinking.

Yes, four years ago, in a referendum, the majority (58 percent) of the American Psychiatric Association supported a decision to remove "homosexuality" from the list of diagnostic labels of mental disorders.

Another 38 percent disapproved that action; so a sizable number of psychiatrists still wish to consider exclusive homosexuality as a mental disorder, even though it is no longer identified as such in the formal diagnostic and statistical manual of the APA.

As far as homosexuality and morality are concerned, a large segment of adherents of fundamentalist and Catholic faiths cite chapter and verse of the Bible or papal edict to mark homosexuality as immoral.

Homosexuality is an emotional issue; and when emotions are aroused, reason falls by the wayside. The current fervor over this issue is far out of proportion to its significance or real scope. It's really somewhat ludicrous to think that an issue like homosexuality will bring out more people to the voting booths than truly serious and significant community matters.

Realistically, homosexuality is nowhere near the potential danger to society or to our children as portrayed in the scare rhetoric of Anita Bryant or Rev. Ron Adrian (who led the Wichita "Concerned Citizens for Community Standards").

As Sigmund Freud observed, students of human nature have long taught us that we are mistaken in regarding our intelligence as an independent force, and in overlooking its dependence upon the emotional life. Nowhere is this more obvious than in discussions about homosexuality, where so many people have their minds made up.

What are some of the facts? Throughout history, societies have given homosexual behavior more or less recognition. The ancient Greeks idealized it. Anthropologists report forty-nine present-day primitive societies accept it in more or less restricted forms; twenty-eight similar cultures condemn the practices.

Kinsey found 60 percent of the men and 33 percent of the women he interviewed admitted some form of homosexual behavior by age forty-five; 37 percent of the men and 13 percent of the women had such an experience after puberty which ended in orgasm. Only 4 percent of Kinsey's respondents identified themselves as exclusively homosexual.

Most students of human sexuality believe that exclusive homosexuality is not inherited, but rather results from conflicts going back to early childhood experiences with mother and father as representative female and male objects. Further, most homosexuals are not so by conscious choice.

Dr. Judd Marmor, former president of the American Psychiatric Association, has summed it up this way:

"Neither homosexual nor heterosexual sex-object choice in human beings is innate or instinctual, but both represent learned behavior. We must conclude that there is nothing inherently sick or unnatural about life experiences that predispose an individual to prefer homosexual sex objects except insofar as this preference represents a socially condemned form of behavior in our culture."

Internal Stress: Aging

"RENEWMENT" INSTEAD OF RETIREMENT

When should you retire?

Should there be a mandatory retirement age, or should the decision be entirely up to you?

These questions have been subject to a good bit of discussion as states and Congress have voted to extend the traditional mandatory retirement age from age sixty-five to seventy. Acually, if it weren't for the costs of living, many people would prefer retiring earlier rather than later.

Whatever age you opt for, if it's more than a few years off, I doubt if you have seriously begun to prepare for it. But you should! Certainly from age forty on, you should be planning ahead for that day.

Most people avoid planning that far ahead because retirement is perceived as preparing to end life. The average person is reluctant to acknowledge the inevitability of aging and death. Yet the increasing life span makes the usual retirement come well ahead of the end of life and presents a great opportunity to explore new horizons.

How could you go about preparing for retirement? Peter Dickinson has an answer for that: *The Complete Retirement Planning Book* (E. P. Dutton).

Dickinson has been in the field of retirement planning for over fifteen years and he retired a couple of years ago at age forty-five!

He describes it this way, "After researching and writing about retirement for over fifteen years, I realized that the prevailing concept governing retirement is all wrong.

"Retirement isn't idleness, letting down or letting go; rather it is a time we can opt for second careers, different life-styles, and new dreams. I don't call it retirement, I call it 'renewment.'"

Dickinson goes further to make a challenge—why wait for a conventional retirement date? Why not start right *now* to prepare for something better?

Some of his straightforward advice:

"It's not *where* you live but *how* you live that determines how much money you need. Simplify your life today and you'll have more money tomorrow.

"Start *now* on a program of enjoyable exercise, proper diet, and sufficient rest, and you'll be happier and healthier today and tomorrow.

"Start *now* to develop a hobby, service project, second career. You can enjoy it today and perfect it tomorrow."

Under "Mistakes Some People Make," Dickinson includes (1) planning too late; (2) planning for too short a time ("you'll probably live longer than you think"); (3) not setting definite goals; (4) not matching goals to personality and temperament; and (5) not spending time to save money.

Overall, I concur with Dickinson's advice to his readers to enjoy a trip through his book, to use it to avoid the pitfalls and to seize the unexpected pleasure of a journey to retirement— "and a life of your choice."

"WHO SAYS THESE REACTIONS ARE
NOT SEVERE?"

Dear Dr. Menninger:

Your comments on menopause contained some statements which I find disturbing. I am female, fifty-five-years old, and I have found the masculine medical view of menopause to be disturbing, nonsupportive and unhelpful.

The phrase: "This period presents physical or emotional problems for only *some two out of every five women," disturbs me. Why the* only? *Two out of five is almost half, and that's a lot of miserable women.*

You also state: "And generally, the physical reactions are not severe—hot flashes, excessive fatigue, feelings of emotional instability." Who says these reactions are not severe? The women or the doctors?

I can state positively that changing from a vibrant, functioning, healthy individual to one who is constantly and excessively fatigued, emotionally disturbed and plagued with hot flashes is most severe. It is devastating!

Coupled with the physical decline is the humiliating knowledge that society as a whole considers the woman less valuable, less desirable and less important during and after menopause. These women are often married to men who are partially or completely impotent, and their lack of interest is considered a failing on the woman's part—not enough kissing, patting and petting.

In fact, the man's lack of sexual interest and/or performance is a contributing factor to the woman's depression. To have you imply that the tired and depressed woman should become a driving sexual force, that it is her duty to entice and charm the impotent man back to his former self is just a bit too much.

Sincerely,
Mrs. G. L.

P.S. The woman who does not enjoy sexual intercourse with her husband is called frigid. Fact—inept husbands are usually the cause. Impotent men are considered pitiful and it is the woman's fault. Fact—impotent husbands are the source of their wives' frustration and misery. It is deadly to be married to an impotent man!

It is true that our society puts a premium on youth. And when you are affected by a distressing condition which doesn't affect everyone, statistics are no consolation. Finally, I can't deny that a doctor's observations may not tell it like you have experienced it.

However, let me refer you—and other women who may also be troubled by the subject of menopause—to a discussion of the subject written by women, in *Our Bodies, Ourselves: A Book by and for Women* prepared by the Boston's Women's Health Collective (Simon & Schuster, New York):

"In our youth-oriented culture, menopause for many people marks a descent into uncool middle and old age . . . Menopause is called 'the change,' and all the implications are that life goes downhill from there . . .

"These views are being changed by women . . . who value

themselves as more than baby machines, who move into middle-age as a welcome time in which they can pursue other kinds of work, who make careful use of drugs available to minimize menopausal discomforts, who learn about ways that good diet, rest and excercise can help prevent problems with menopause."

Our Bodies, Ourselves discusses far more than just menopause. It addresses a wide range of topics of concern to women of all ages. A number of women have advised me that they believe this is one book every woman should have.

Incidentally, your "facts" about the frigid woman and the impotent husband may be true in some cases, but not all. The causes of sexual dysfunction in both men and women are rarely so simple. Most often, the problems result from a combination of both inner emotional conflicts and tensions in a couple's relationships.

ABUSE OF THE ELDERLY—WHY?

It was the kind of news that makes your stomach turn.

Someone had broken into an apartment shared by two elderly women and had brutally beaten them. The assailant left them unconscious, with broken jaws and disfigured faces, to be discovered later by neighbors.

Everyone who heard about the incident was appalled. Why? How could someone do such violence upon harmless and benign folks? What could motivate such behavior?

Robbery? The apartment had been ransacked, but only a small amount of money was stolen; other cash in the apartment was untouched. Similarly, only one or two pieces of jewelry were taken.

What else could prompt such senseless violence? The intensity of the attack suggests a considerable explosion of rage, which you might speculate stems from past frustrations at the hands of "older" people.

In psychiatric consultation, patients often describe childhood experiences of hurt and frustration at the hands of older people in their lives—most often parents, but sometimes teachers and others. For most children, those hurts are balanced and resolved by parental love and other compensations. But not for all.

In the past few years, there has been an increasing awareness of the number of children who have experienced considerable physical abuse at the hands of their parents. These children realize that attempts to strike back against an abusing parent only result in greater punishment.

Their resentments thus accumulate and fester; and they remain within, ticking like a time bomb, until triggered to an explosion at some later date.

Of course, elderly people are more frail, less agile, and thus they have always been more vulnerable to criminal assault. As symbolic parental figures, they are also ready scapegoats for the unresolved hostility and aggression some people have for their parents.

For generations, elderly people have been the targets of harrassment by teenagers and young adults. Adolescents, both as individuals and together in a gang, will often pick on an older person to taunt them and play pranks on them.

There does appear to have been an increase in the number of violent attacks on elderly people. Of course, there are more elderly people these days, more people living longer, increasing the population at risk.

But there's more to these attacks than just more senior citizens. Professor Suzanne Steinmetz of the University of Delaware has presented findings of research on household violence to congressional committees. She reported that elderly Americans are suffering more beatings directly from their own children.

She cites a number of cases: An alcoholic man tied his eighty-nine-year-old father to a chair whenever the old man refused to hand over his Social Security check; a thirteen-year-old girl beat up her seventy-eight-year-old grandmother; the list was endless.

Professor Steinmetz cites increasing conflict between the needs of parents and the goals of their children as one cause for this violence. And she predicts an increase in the amount of violence children use to control elderly parents unless adequate support systems are available for the elderly.

A FATAL MOVE

Several years ago, following the death of my wife's mother, we were faced with helping my wife's eighty-five-year-old father decide where he could best live. He was in fairly good health, but he was filled with doubts about remaining alone. He also wasn't sure about moving north after twenty years in Florida.

As it turned out, he came to live in a retirement home near us. And the adjustment in his style of living was no mean feat. After you've functioned independently all your life in your own home, it's quite a struggle to adapt to an institutional life.

Though he's had some rough moments, he's survived and is still going strong. But in view of his experience, I was particularly interested in a report by Norman Bourestrom and Leon Pastalan of a project carried out by the Institute of Gerontology at the University of Michigan.

These researchers and their staff spent two years studying what happens to elderly patients in nursing homes when they are relocated to different settings. They started their project after becoming aware of the considerable number of elderly who were forced to relocate.

Often, the relocation is prompted by economic pressures or policy changes. Sometimes the move is forced by the closing of an inadequate nursing home. Rarely is the relocation made with concern for the individual patient's welfare.

178

In all the cases studied by Bourestrom and Pastalan, the facilities to which the patients were transferred provided medical, nutritional and nursing care that was equal to or better than the care available in the previous facility.

Despite that fact, the researchers found that the relocation was likely to be a fatal move. The death rates for those persons whose situation was radically changed were double the death rate of a control group which did not change.

Further, the study of the survivors in the radical change group showed other destructive effects. These patients grew increasingly pessimistic about their health. They withdrew from activities in which they formerly engaged. They were less inclined to trust the staff looking after them, or to feel that others were interested in them.

While the relocation had a negative effect on all age groups, it was most harmful for those of very advanced age. More than half of the patients over seventy-eight years of age in the radical change group died, while only 28 percent of their counterparts in the control group died.

One intriguing finding was that relocation tended to be more traumatic for women than men. Although the researchers could not be precisely sure why this was so, they speculated that women become more involved and dependent upon their immediate environment.

Elderly persons who were able to openly express feelings of resentment and anger were more likely to survive. Those who retreated from conflict situations by denying their anger had a death rate twice that of persons who expressed anger openly.

Since the effects of relocation on the death rates tended to be concentrated just prior to and following the move, the researchers concluded that planning and preparation of elderly persons

179

for such a relocation should be careful and thorough. It should begin as soon as possible before the move and continue at least three months afterward.

In a pilot premove preparation program, deaths were reduced. The Gerontology Institute therefore developed a plan to help relocate nursing home patients which was utilized by the state of Pennsylvania. Their plan is one which can be helpful to anyone who has an elderly relative in prospect of moving.

SOME THOUGHTS ON FACING DEATH

Dear Dr. Menninger:

Recently, you wrote concerning reactions to the death of a family member. The trauma of death in the family has changed the personalities of many. Some become bitter and hateful; others may react with consideration and compassion.

In any case, death of a loved one seldom leaves a life unchanged.

Death is a natural occurrence when it happens to someone else. It is a terrifying thought to every human being until he has resolved the question in his own mind and conscience.

Whether it is a child of seven or a man of seventy, he faces the trauma of his own personal death. The questions: "Why am I here? Where will I go when I die?"

Death should be the number one topic of conversation for the total populace, because we are the generation living in the nuclear age. The late President Kennedy phrased it thus, "The sword of Damocles now hangs over our head."

Elizabeth Kubler Ross has received very favorable recognition for her book, Death and Dying. *Among medical and some college students, the topic of death is being discussed more freely.*

Please comment on facing death.

Sincerely,
Mrs. R. H., Iowa

Since mankind does have instruments like the hydrogen bomb which can bring about our total destruction, it does seem reasonable that we all think about how we might face death. However these are also times when we have increased skills for preserving and sustaining life.

In the past fifty years, the average life span has increased by 30 percent. In 1920, the average life expectancy at birth was just over fifty-four years; now it is over seventy.

Yet, death is inevitable, and there is no easy way to face death. With few exceptions, no one likes to anticipate dying. And when it actually approaches, most people will not be ready for it.

Faith can be an extremely important source of sustenance when facing death, along with a capacity to face one's feelings.

An increasing number of books and papers have been written on death and dying, describing feelings and experiences. These writings may be helpful not only for self-understanding, but they may help those who go on living to come to grips with the death of their loved ones.

In addition to Kubler Ross, let me call attention to two other books which present a somewhat different perspective of death, and which address your questions.

One is *Death and the College Student,* edited by Edwin Shneidman, Ph.D. (Behavioral Publications, New York, 1972). It is a collection of nineteen brief essays on death and suicide written by Harvard undergraduates enrolled in a course on the psychology of death taught by Dr. Shneidman.

182

In a foreword, the former director of the Harvard Student Health Service, Dr. Dana Farnsworth, writes, "Any student of the way human beings deal with tragedy and the prospect of their own nonexistence will find this book both stimulating and illuminating."

The second is *Life After Life,* by Dr. Raymond Moody (Mockingbird Books).

Originally educated in philosophy and now a physician, Dr. Moody encountered a number of persons who had what he calls "near death experiences." Subsequently, he has collected narratives from over one hundred persons.

From the mass of narratives, he has identified a composite experience, with some fifteen separate elements which recur again and again in people's experiences. These include such things as feelings of peace and quiet, being in a dark tunnel, being out of the body, meeting other spiritual beings, and a quality of being unable to express what happened.

In nearly every case, he notes, "the experience affects one's life profoundly, especially his views about death and its relationship to life."

External Stress: People

AN EYE FOR AN EYE...

Rare is the child who is not, at some point in growing up, confronted with a bully who threatens him or beats him up. What do you advise the child to do? Fight back? Turn the other cheek? When is discretion the better part of valor?

Those are tough questions, and there are no easy answers. It is predictable, however, that unless one person is overwhelmingly more powerful, hitting back is most likely to lead to a continuing conflict.

Evidence for that is in the daily news reports from Northern Ireland and the Middle East. Repeatedly, extremists there exchange "an eye for an eye" in ever-escalating terror and destruction that appear absolutely beyond control. It seems senseless and endless. Thus in Northern Ireland one winter night, extremist Protestants invaded two Catholic households and killed five men at their dinner tables. The following night, Catholics stopped a busload of Protestant textile workers on the way home from work and executed ten.

This retaliatory practice is deeply rooted, not only in the history of civilization, but also in the beginnings of our personality. And if we are to survive as a civilization, we need to understand it and more effectively control it.

"Retaliation" is derived from the Latin, "talio," which means reciprocal punishment in kind. The principle of the talion has been traced to early Babylonian law. There it was determined criminals should receive as punishment exactly those injuries and damages they had inflicted on their victims.

The Book of Exodus relates that Moses, on Mount Sinai, received from God not only the Ten Commandments but also a guide for punishments. Included were "life for life, eye for eye, tooth for tooth." And in early Palestine many injuries and thefts were not considered wrongs against the state, but "private" wrongs to be settled between the injured party and the one who inflicted the injury.

In Palestine and Rome, the law was gradually modified, so that instead of exact retribution, organ for organ, the injured person could claim the value of what was lost. A system of fines developed to supplant the *lex talionis*. Nevertheless, vestiges of the law of the talion have persisted in various forms to this day, like the death penalty for murder (where it is still practiced).

In recent times, exact eye-for-an-eye retaliation has been practiced more by citizens operating outside the law. Gang wars, vigilante groups and terrorist groups have all practiced the law of the talion, feeling that they cannot trust the system of justice to exact proper punishment of offenders. Of these groups, the terrorists have been especially prone to make indiscriminate retaliations, killing and injuring innocent, uninvolved citizens in their acts of retribution.

The roots of this behavior are evident in the infant and young child and may be readily observed in children at play. When the child is hurt or frustrated, he experiences an intense wish to strike back. If he cannot readily identify who has hurt him, that powerful impulse to strike back will be expressed indiscriminately.

This retaliatory impulse is a powerful emotional force which lies deep in everyone's personality, activated by being hurt or wronged. It is not necessarily rational. And as we grow up, all too often we go ahead and strike back, later using elaborate rationalizations to justify our behavior.

Obviously, for people to live comfortably with one another, we can't simply retaliate whenever we're hurt. We do have to learn to tolerate some pain and disappointment without retribution. And we must realize that exacting an eye for an eye or a life for a life only perpetuates rage and more hurt. Hate begets more hate.

VIOLENCE IN THE HOME

"What can you do?"

A physician-friend was posing that question to me about a recent case he had—a woman had called him for help with her emotionally upset husband who had been beating her.

The woman felt her husband needed psychiatric help, and so did the doctor. But the husband was reluctant to get help, and his wife couldn't force him to do so. The police were reluctant to intervene unless she would sign a formal complaint against her husband, and she didn't want to do that.

Her dilemma is not uncommon. In the past few years, along with an increased awareness of problems of child abuse, there has been greater recognition of the extent of spouse abuse.

One questionnaire of 385 college students revealed that 16 percent reported violence between their parents within the year.

Another study compared families suspected by authorities of being violent with a control group of their neighbors. Over half of the "suspect" group admitted one or more spouse assaults. More startling, however, was the finding that one-third of the "control" group of neighbors also did so!

More recently, a research study in Kalamazoo, Michigan, estimated that 10 percent of the families in the community have experienced some form of violence between marriage partners.

The Kalamazoo study was reported earlier in the *Social Case-*

work Journal, a publication of the Family Service Association of America. The report was authored by Professor John Flynn of the School of Social Work at Western Michigan University.

Some other findings of the Kalamazoo study: In nonfatal assaults, the victim is almost always female and the assaulter male. Presumably because of the husband's greater physical strength, when women become violent, they use weapons, which frequently lead to more serious injuries and death.

Homicide statistics reveal that when a spouse is killed, the victim is male as often as female. Thus, though more men may be assaulters, the women are more dangerous when they are the aggressors.

Most studies have shown that a substantial proportion of participants in marital violence have witnessed it during their childhood taking place between their parents. Further, in Kalamazoo, two-fifths of the assaulters had been abused as children.

Professor Flynn observed that families with violence were often families under stress from one or more sources—financial problems, health and employment problems, conflicts over children or the marriage.

Victims of assault attributed the actions of the spouse to mental illness, alcohol abuse and/or extreme jealousy. In addition, the assaulter often had expectations of the victim which were not being met, such as the wife not changing her personality to suit the husband, not being submissive to his will, or not coping well enough with family problems.

The assaults follow a common pattern. Generally, the incident starts with a verbal argument, at which the woman is often better in gaining the upper hand. To dominate the situation, the man becomes physical, and the escalation is frequently associated with excessive use of alcohol.

What can you do? In Kalamazoo, almost all the victims did seek help from one or another resource—police, clergy, marriage counselors. Few of the husbands were willing to participate in counseling. And often divorce failed to solve the problem; some husbands continue to seek out their former wives to assault them.

Flynn found that few community resources were ready to deal with wife beating as a problem. Frequently, community attitudes support or even approve of wife beating. Where others view the action as wrong, they have doubts about interfering with a "family matter."

The result is that the victim is in a kind of double bind situation. If she seeks help, she may end up getting little help from the community agencies. At the same time, by doing so she may provoke an additional violent reaction from her spouse.

HOW MANY GOOD SAMARITANS ARE THERE?

You may have heard the story. In the midst of a winter blizzard in Iowa, a young woman driving alone skidded off a country road. Unable to move her car, she started walking toward the nearest dwelling.

When she knocked on the farmhouse door, a voice answered through the door telling her to go away. She struggled to the next farmhouse. The same thing happened. It happened yet a third time before she was spotted by a bus driver.

Because she was not dressed for the elements, she had already suffered some frostbite. She was saved from a worse fate by the good samaritan action of the bus driver.

She was quoted by reporters as planning to return, when the weather was better, to the farms where she had sought refuge to ask the folks, "Why?"

In recent years, the reluctance of people to be good samaritans and become "involved" when others cry for help has been well publicized. Most widely reported was the 1964 rape-murder of Kitty Genovese in New York City. There not one of thirty-eight people who heard or saw what was going on did anything to help.

Almost everyone has been in a position of being stranded and needing help sometime in life. I recall running out of gas at one o'clock in the morning on a turnpike. Ten or twelve of the few cars on the road at that hour whizzed by until one pulled over.

In it, a young man was traveling with his wife and two small children; the backseat was full of belongings. He had stopped in spite of his wife's protestation that he shouldn't; the argument continued until I got in. And he gave me a lift to the next interchange.

Most people don't like to think of themselves as "uncaring." Most say they would help someone in distress. Yet, not all actually do, and there are different reasons why. The two most striking are fear of the stranger and a personal commitment of higher priority.

Think of the last time you were driving down the road and saw a car stranded. You may have given a prayer of thanks that it wasn't you, as you drove on. You were late for an appointment or committed to something that didn't allow for any time out to help others.

Besides, you probably assumed that someone else would help. Or the police or highway patrol would stop as part of their job. They are more prepared to cope with emergencies, anyway.

In addition, you may have had sufficient look at the car and the people to have doubts about whether you could trust them. Fear of the stranger is a powerful deterrent to helping, despite the fact that this fear is generally out of proportion to reality. The vast majority of people seeking help are not robbers or rapists or murderers.

Yet another perspective on this dilemma is offered by three psychologists at the City University of New York. Writing in *Psychology Today*, they reported reactions to a "lost" child asking for help in several large cities and small towns.

Less than half (46 percent) of the large city dwellers responded with an offer to help a lost child; nearly three-fourths (72 percent) of the small town folks did. And in the small towns, even those who didn't help were usually sympathetic.

In the big cities, most who refused to help "did so abruptly," ignoring the child, swerving, sidestepping. Others, with hardly a pause, put some money in the child's hand and moved on.

Not all the large cities were the same. Boston and Philadelphia were most unsympathetic—two-thirds refused to help. In New York City, it was fifty-fifty. In Chicago, two-thirds helped.

The researchers concluded that the more people around, the less likely people are to help. They assume someone else will respond and they excuse themselves from any responsibility. Also, the city dweller learns to ignore demands on his time and attention.

Of course, that doesn't explain the actions of the farm folks in the Iowa blizzard. I suspect they were simply afraid.

External Stress: Marriage, Divorce, Widowhood

WHY GET MARRIED?

An increasing number of couples are living together without the benefit of marriage. From 1960 to 1970, census figures showed a twenty-fold increase in young adults living with an unrelated member of the opposite sex. Since 1970, the number has again doubled.

Why so? Why a reluctance to make a permanent marriage commitment to one another? Some young people rationalize their behavior by saying they're not ready. They don't want to get married until they are "sure." Sure of what? Not being left? Or hurt? Or trapped?

One of the significant features of the marriage contract is an agreement to accept each other "for better or for worse, for richer or for poorer, in sickness and in health." There is no guarantee against being hurt.

Why get married? Recently, I received another letter from Helen Graebner, a widow in Grandview, Missouri, who speaks to this question beautifully:

Dear Dr. Menninger:

I wonder if you will sometime write on the positive aspects of marriage. It seems to me that marriage has had a "bad press" for quite some time now. We seem to read almost exclusively about the negative qualities of marriage.

Divorce or "living together" without a commitment are the fashionable things to do.

I think that the closest, finest, most satisfying relationship in the world is that found between a husband and wife in a good marriage. And I believe this relationship can be found only within marriage. Which, I suppose, marks me as hopelessly old-fashioned; but I still believe it.

I am aware that the term "good" does not necessarily mean the same thing to all people. I am speaking of a relationship in which each partner cares more for the happiness of the other than for his or her own. Within that context, a caring, loving concerned relationship can banish loneliness and illuminate the dailyness of living.

My husband and I had that kind of marriage; it is not achieved easily or quickly and must be earned by constant effort—but it is worth all it costs in energy and time and thought and love expended.

I am appalled at much of the drivel being written in today's books and slick magazines: do what you want to do—never mind whom you hurt in the process; find yourself.

In the first place, no one ever "found" a self; you build one, little by little, day by day, year by year. In the second place, it is only a child who believes that he can always do only what he wants to do.

A mature person knows that sometimes the needs of others must take precedence over his or her own desires of the moment. Who wants to get up in the middle of the night with a sick or fretful child?

What the please-yourself authors are not telling their readers is that their way leads eventually to aloneness and loneliness. The Christian edict that you gain a life by losing it is still valid—not losing it in slavery or servitude to a mate, but in blending it into a partnership to seek common goals.

This does not mean that each one must sacrifice his or her own personality; each partner's concern for the other will make opportunities for that personality to develop.

I am sad when I think of all the people who are being cheated of a wonderful loving relationship within a marriage because they listen to and believe the antimarriage propaganda so prevalent today.

The horrible thought is that most of these people are going to grow into a lonely old age. So, please, Dr. Menninger, write from time to time on the positive, wonderful aspects of marriage.

Sincerely,
Helen Graebner

IN SUPPORT OF "THE PIECE OF PAPER"— MARRIAGE

Dear Dr. Menninger,
How about an article for the marriage contract. Please give us parents some good arguments for marriage other than the moral issues.

Several of my friends have been disarmed when their offspring say, "It's just a piece of paper (the marriage certificate); we don't need it." Surely society offers many benefits for people entering into this written agreement.

You surely don't need my help, but I felt better listing some of the benefits. I've put them down in the following made-up letter:

Dear Mary!
"I finally told my parents we would be living together. Boy! Were they uptight! I explained we'll be just as married and true to each other as they are, except for 'the piece of paper.'

"This way, we can pull out if it's not working, and nobody gets hurt; there's no hassle with a divorce. Don't worry, they'll accept you in time because they love me, and I'm their son.

There are just a few things we'll have to iron out along the way—like, do I introduce you as my girl or my wife?

And do we sign Mr. and Mrs. on anything? I'm not sure.

"My job pays pretty good. So long as I don't get laid off, we'll be just fine. I know my unemployment benefits won't cover you and the boy. And if you should be taken ill, my sick benefits won't cover you either. But we'll get by okay.

"It's too bad we can't get a cheaper rate of insurance on your car (a second car usually does), but I don't think they'll give us this break. Who needs it?

"Trust me, Mary. I have even the most serious situations figured out. God forbid anything terrible happening, but should one of us need written permission for surgery, I can call your folks, or you, mine. Since we're not married, they can't accept our signing for each other. But don't worry, we'll look out for each other.

"It probably would be a good idea someday to let our folks know our wishes, should the ultimate occur. If one of us gets killed, I know what kind of funeral you would like, and you for me. But we may have no say so in these matters, since we are not man and wife on paper.

"I think I have covered everything here, as we must look at all phases in an adult manner.

"Meanwhile, I can't wait to move in with you and Johnny. It will be great for the boy, too. He'll have a kind-of-a-father again, even if I can't sign his report card to show him how proud I am of him. He's quite a boy; and I know if this doesn't work out, he'll adjust as he did before. After all, a father for even awhile is better than none at all, right?"

Love,
Bill

Your letter from Bill to Mary covers many small practical issues;

but those points may or may not "score" with them. The bottom line is really the kind of commitment they plan to make to one another.

Most people want to have their cake and eat it too. That is, they want the best of both worlds—the freedom to do your own thing, the security of a constant relationship. Maturation involves facing up to a compromise in those objectives; and in a good marriage, you achieve the ideal compromise.

Although some couples may make a private contract in a living together arrangement, there is value in the making of a public commitment to one another. That is part of the marriage ceremony.

Even if you don't get married, you should not assume you can avoid being hurt if the relationship doesn't work out. There may be a wish to limit their relationship and avoid entanglement, but increasingly, living together arrangements have involved significant legal and emotional ties.

THE "SEVEN YEAR ITCH"

Is there really such a thing as a "Seven Year Itch"?

That's a condition of increased marital restlessness and tension in one or both partners after roughly seven years of marriage. There may be an increase in extramarital sex (or fantasies of such activity), thoughts of separations and of changing one's life-style, and general marital dissatisfaction without apparent cause.

The Seven Year Itch label comes from a 1950s play of that title. In it, after seven faithful years, the husband is bored and restless and becomes involved with other women. While the play focused on the restlessness of the husband, wives are just as vulnerable.

Drs. Ellen Berman, William Miller, Neville Vines and Harold Lief, at the Marriage Council of Philadelphia, decided to check out whether there really is something like the Seven Year Itch. So they surveyed the population of couples seeking help at their clinic for marriage counseling.

They discovered that the greatest number of couples seeking help have at least one member in the twenty-seven to thirty-two-year-old age range; and the average duration of the marriage for those couples was seven years!

They concluded, "The significantly greater frequency for couples in the age group twenty-seven to thirty-two, married seven years, suggested that the Seven Year Itch is more than just a figure of speech."

These marriages were not, however, characterized so much by boredom as by the same kinds of long-standing problems found in the clinic's population as a whole—problems in communication and the sexual relationship.

What then was different about these couples? Most often, the request for help was made by one member of the couple who was going through some sort of personal crisis and reassessment of himself or herself.

Berman and her associates equated this crisis to a kind of "age-thirty crisis," which other investigators have also described, and which may occur anywhere from age twenty-seven to thirty-two. At this period in life, the person makes his or her first reassessment of life goals and life-style.

The kinds of feelings expressed have to do with changing one's self-image and developing a new view of the world and the future. Some of the statements made by these people:

"I'm a different person now, with different needs."

"If I don't change now, I'll be stuck forever, and I'm getting old."

"I woke up one morning and decided I had stood this long enough."

Although many of the studies of transition periods in life have been of men, Berman notes that women go through the same kind of painful reevaluation. A woman's transition may be particularly difficult if she has spent the years of her twenties closeted at home with small children.

Often a precipitating event—the death of a friend, or a new relationship—prompts a sense of restlessness and a need for reevaluation on the part of one or both members of the marital couple. When there is some degree of marital conflict already present, this restlessness makes it worse.

In working with these couples, Berman and her associates help them to see the struggles as part of "an orderly and predictable stage" of maturation. The outcome of this transitional stage can be a dissolution of the marriage, or it may return the marriage to a much stronger and more solid footing.

To understand the period as a life crisis, Gail Sheehy's bestseller, *Passages,* is sometimes recommended. It discusses life crises in a popular style, although Berman finds her examples, in many instances, to be oversimplified.

Trial separations commonly occur in these couples, as a means to check out the fantasies of an alternate life-style. But, as Berman notes, "Brief separation may provide a vacation from a spouse but seldom a real taste of a new life structure."

"THE FASTEST-GROWING DISEASE
IN OUR COUNTRY"

Dear Dr. Menninger:

I've been going to write you for some time. It seems like life has so many problems along the way, and at middle-age they haven't been any less. We live in a small town in rural America. Not Peyton Place, but I'm beginning to wonder.

There are so many husbands and wives cheating on each other. Some of these people are really great church-goers and have many good qualities. I hope they will see themselves in this letter and wake up before they destroy another marriage.

Romance in an affair is not like being married. Marriage has so many responsibilities, and living with someone else is never easy. If you have problems now, divorce and remarriage should add a few more. What is it going to do to all the children involved?

A husband and wife have a commitment to each other. We can't be perfect but there are all kinds of ways to improve a marriage and become happier people. There are mental health centers for counseling, all kinds of books available (and the best of all is still the Bible—read what First Corinthians 13:4-8 has to say about love).

When was the last time you really communicated with

202

each other? Do you prepare good meals for your family? Is the house presentable? Do you relax at home together? Share some common interests? Do you care how your children turn out?

I feel divorce is one of the fastest-growing diseases in our country, so please discuss this.

Mrs. A.

Divorce is increasingly common in this country; in recent years, the number of divorces has exceeded millions.

Why does one become involved in an extramarital affair? Is it because of lack of satisfaction in the marriage? Is it a lack of will power? Is it anger toward the spouse? It may be all of these. Rarely is there a simple and easy explanation.

Often the emotional interactions are quite complex. It may be easy to criticize the behavior from a distance, but usually there is more than meets the eye. We don't really understand why one person is attracted to another. Sometimes circumstances set a person up for an unexpected emotional involvement that seems to occur without conscious intent.

Some people do seem to take their marriage commitment lightly. Marriage has its frustrations as well as its satisfactions, and a romantic affair without the burdens of a marital contract can be most seductive. It takes effort to continue to cope with the frustrations, particularly when the romantic halo wears off.

In all human relationships, there are mixed feelings. Even in the most loving partnership, there are times when friction develops. You're in trouble when the periods of friction outlast the periods of affection and love. It is up to each couple to recognize their limits and to determine when the argument or turmoil or lack of continuing affection means they would be better off separated.

Divorce does introduce significant problems of its own. Splitting up is always a painful process, often more so for one partner than the other. Yet, there are times when a divorce can be the best decision for a couple to make. And when it is truly the best decision, the children can adjust to it.

DIVORCE DOESN'T HAVE TO BE A BAD SCENE

Dear Dr. Menninger:

I've read so much on the "poor deprived children" that come from "broken" homes, I figured that it was time for me to say something. What I wonder is how in the world these psychologists can express all their opinions. I mean, do they know what it's like? Were their parents divorced?

My parents were divorced when I was seven years old. Half of my friends' parents have been divorced. None of them has suffered any great traumas from it. Talking from experience, having your parents get divorced is a lot better than living in a tense, violent atmosphere.

People make mistakes and divorce is a correction. I'm fourteen now and my mother remarried a few years ago. It wasn't always easy, but it's better than if they had stayed together. The only thing I missed was not always having my father around. But I think we have a better relationship now, anyway.

Also, parents don't always seek revenge. My mom and dad and stepdad get along fine. If people didn't regard divorce as a bad scene, it wouldn't be one.

Sincerely,
S. S.

It is good that you have been able to experience the positive side of your parents' divorce. It is true that many psychologists and psychiatrists have strong opinions about the trauma some children experience. But their views are sometimes the result of seeing some of the "casualties," those kids who don't make it as well as you have.

One of the best studies of children in divorced families is the work done by Judith Wallerstein and Joan Kelly in the San Francisco Bay area. They have followed 131 children over several years. And they have found that some have adjusted quite well. Yet there are a number who have had quite a struggle, and there are rough spots for everyone.

The adolescent youngsters they interviewed were able to adjust best when the parents permitted the child to keep out of their struggle. Where that happened, the youngster was more able to realistically look at both parents and to feel some compassion for them.

Sometimes, one parent in the midst of a marital crisis tries to use the children as a lever against the other. Or, preoccupied with his or her concerns, the parent may be unable to attend to the concerns of the child.

"NOW I JUST DON'T KNOW WHAT TO DO"

Dear Dr. Menninger:

After reading columns mentioning help for depression, I decided to write you. I lost my wonderful husband four years ago after forty-three years of marriage. Within five years, I lost also my mother, mother-in-law, father and counselor.

I tried several volunteer jobs, but they did nothing for me. Now I just don't know what to do. Loneliness is like a disease; memories, even good ones, make me sad. I feel lost. If you can suggest any reading material that will help, I will be happy to look it up.

Respectfully,
F. K.

At the same time I received your letter, I received a marvelous testimonial from Helen Graebner of Grandview, Missouri, herself a widow for over five years. She offers some excellent suggestions which she hopes might be shared to help others. Indeed, she wrote that writing the letter "pulled me out of a bad day." Some of her thoughts:

"It's true that the loneliness does not get better with time; we can learn to live with it, but we need to work at it constantly.

"After the first days and weeks when your friends and family rally around to comfort and help you, they become increasingly busy with their own lives and you are left more to yourself. They do not understand the feelings and despair and loneliness that you are experiencing. The terrible trauma, the absolute finality, the ending of part of your life which comes with the death of a husband or wife cannot be imagined.

"Since no one else can do it for you, you must get back to living. No matter how difficult, get involved with your life again. Your friends may hesitate to invite you to dinners or gatherings at their homes. Widows bother people. We make them uneasy. They don't know what to say or do when we are around.

"Do something about it. You invite friends to your house for dinner, or bridge, or whatever you have been accustomed to. But invite at least two couples. Then the lack of a host is not so apparent.

"Get busy and do things outside the empty house. If you have a job, fine. If you have marketable skills, use them. Or volunteer. Teach a Sunday School class, or work in a church group, scouts, hospitals, Red Cross. I've discovered that the best way to forget my own unhappiness is to do something for someone else.

"Books are also one of my biggest helps—all kinds of books, historical fiction, mysteries, biographies. Much of it is pure escape reading, but why not? It gets me over the terrible times when the empty house seems about to collapse on me.

"The book which has done the most for me, and which I reread often, is *Man's Search for Meaning* by Dr. Victor Frankl.

"Beware of self-pity. It is addictive and as destructive as drugs. And be careful not to become a babbler, a talker-without-stopping.

"Do what you want to do; go where you want to go. Take a college course or an adult study course. Learn new skills. If you can afford it, travel is wonderful; and it need not be expensive, either. Take a bus trip around our country.

"Most important of all, prayer will always help. I could never have made it this far without God's help. Just ask Him.

"You will get so tired of doing everything for yourself! Everything. Carrying in the groceries, paying the bills, putting on your own car license plates, going places by yourself. But you can also take pride in your ability to do everything. My motto is, 'What I have to do, I can.'

"I realized one day that I have children and grandchildren and many friends who love me. They love me very much. I'm not their first love—their own families have to be first—but altogether it adds up to a lot of love. And I'm grateful for it.

"Add up the love in your life. And be glad for it."

ONE WIDOW'S PROTECTION
AGAINST DEPRESSION

Dear Dr. Menninger:

Regarding a letter from a widow I saw recently, I too am a widow of one year. And the holidays have taken their toll, as my husband died Christmas day one year ago. I seem to have reached a plateau of being alone and lonely as I feel that no one cares, what's the use? And I feel the utter hopelessness of it all!

I was left without any funds and do have to work to survive, so that seems to be my salvation. But it means nothing otherwise. I just go through each day, one by one, and miss my Beloved more each day.

I just seem to shut myself away from everyone and cannot get interested in anything. I don't seem to care. After thirty-six years of having someone care, it's hard to adjust.

Sincerely,
F. Z., California

Your continuing depression in response to the loss of your spouse of thirty-six years is not unusual. What is particularly significant, however, is your "salvation" by working.

In December, a *Newsweek* cover story on women at work pointed out that nearly 48 percent of all the women in this country now hold jobs or are actively looking for gainful employment. However, in all the discussion of the rewards of work for women, there has been little mention of its value as a protection against severe depression.

Of course, working women can become depressed. But studies have found a lower prevalence of depression in older women who work. Those studies prompted some investigators with the Depression Unit of the Yale University School of Medicine Department of Psychiatry to compare depression in working women and housewives.

There is a logic to a job providing some protection against depression. Depression is an inward turning of aggressive feelings—anger, resentment—which cannot be comfortably or appropriately expressed toward any outside object. For example, it's hard to blame anyone or anything for your husband's death; so you must absorb those feelings of distress.

Work provides a socially acceptable opportunity to express some aggressive energies outwardly. In addition, work usually occurs in a setting where you can get some support and appreciation from other people, to partially compensate for the lost object.

In their study, the Yale investigators matched a group of depressed housewives with a group of depressed working women. They followed both groups over a period of several months of antidepressant therapy.

They noted that the working women seemed more depressed when they first sought help, but they tended to recover faster than did the housewives. Although both groups had improved after four weeks of therapy, the improvement was more marked for the workers.

In addition, the working women felt more competent, were

less frequently bored in their free time, and were more at ease in social situations than were the housewives.

The Yale findings thus confirmed the assumption that working offers women some protection against and some distraction from depression. Accordingly, a woman who is depressed should be encouraged to continue at her job if she works. The structure and the diversion of her work may well contribute to her recovery.

External Stress: Children

A CHOICE—TO DESIRE PARENTHOOD OR NOT

Dear Dr. Menninger:

A letter from a woman who was "deathly afraid of having a baby" prompts me to write you. As I read the letter, I felt bombarded by the personal pronouns "I, me, my, myself."

I went back and counted these pronouns, and they were used thirty-two times; baby or child was mentioned thirteen times; husband was mentioned eight times. Seldom have I read a letter which I felt exhibited such self-centeredness.

I wonder if the fear of having a baby physically is more what it will "deprive" her of, such as her job. She doesn't want anything to interfere with her present "life-style" as she wants to live it.

This makes it look as though her fear of having a baby physically is an excuse. She doesn't want the baby, and therefore she is even depriving her husband of his rights for a satisfactory sex life.

She may also feel that the baby could deprive her of some of her husband's love and attention which he might lavish on a child.

This is something she should face squarely.

Mrs. V. W., Iowa

Dear Dr. Menninger:

I must disagree with your anwer to the woman who did not want children. You spoke of these feelings as "irrational fears." Have you never heard of the choice people have to make whether they desire parenthood or not?

More and more people are opting for nonparenthood after realizing the economic as well as social hardships children bring. Your response to her letter showed nothing short of what is called pronatalism.

Parenthood is not an inborn desire, but a learned response which is unfortunately taught with such force that up to now, few have questioned it. But this woman is obviously happy with her job, and it is the husband who is in need of counseling. His egotistical need to "reproduce himself" is a dangerous problem.

I am a member of NON—National Organization for Nonparents. I speak with many women who feel guilty about their desire to stay childless among all this pronatalism.

The thousands of abused children that are beaten or abandoned each year are proof that overcoming her fears is not the answer to the problem.

Sincerely,
Mrs. A. Q., California

Your reactions to the same letter (from Mrs. B. I.) reflect different feelings about having children. It is true that an increasing number of couples these days are making a conscious and rational decision not to have children.

They are doing so for good reasons—the population explosion and their own careers.

I suspect I do have a "pronatalism" bias. My wife and I have six children, a goal we set before the "Population Bomb" was so publicized.

Our children have given us many satisfactions, along with frustrations and disappointments. Certainly child raising takes time and energy which has to come from somewhere. Inevitably, there is a dilution of the attention between husband and wife with third, fourth or more parties (children) around.

At the same time, there is a special challenge in bringing forth new beings who gradually establish their own identity and who search for unique ways to carry on in life—not as extensions of us, but as separate and individual persons doing their own thing.

This is no small challenge; and it should be assumed willingly, enthusiastically, and jointly by both parents. Couples who don't feel they want to have children thus shouldn't be forced or shamed into doing so.

YOUNG AND OLD DIFFER IN ATTITUDES TOWARD CHILDREN

Ann Landers created a bit of a stir when she reported a reader-ship survey on attitudes toward children. Seventy percent of her respondents said that they would not have children again; some did so with surprising and intense bitterness.

To assess the attitudes more accurately in their area, the *Kansas City Star* carried out its own survey. Using a carefully developed questionnaire, the paper made phone interviews with 409 randomly selected citizens.

Their findings were in stark contrast with the Landers' report: 94 percent of the parents surveyed in Kansas City said they would have children over again.

The *Star* invited me to review their findings and comment. Interestingly enough, there was little difference in the responses tabulated by sex. Men and women agreed almost completely. Only in one statement was the result a little unexpected.

One might assume that women would be most concerned about being restricted by having children. Yet, only 37 percent of the women felt their personal freedom was restricted by having children; 48 percent of the men did!

The most remarkable findings in the survey come from a review of the responses from different age groups. Careful perusal of these data suggests attitudes change as people grow older. This is particularly evident in responses to the statement, "a woman needs to have a family to be happy." Overall, 34 percent of the people surveyed agreed with this statement; 64 percent disagreed.

Considered by age grouping, the agreement with that statement increases progressively with increasing age: from one out of five (20 percent) of the eighteen to twenty-four-year-olds, to one out of two (49 percent) of the senior citizens over age sixty-five.

These responses suggest that as one ages, one senses an increasing importance to having children and a family. The same impression is given by the overwhelming number (81 percent) of respondents sixty-five and older who felt children didn't restrict their freedom. Indeed, when you are that old, you may often find children are the means by which your freedom is actually increased, helping you to get out and around.

In some ways, however, older people are more skeptical about children. Two-fifths (40 percent) of the sixty-five and older group felt that "when children start their own home, they tend to ignore or forget about parents." Only 45 percent of the older age group, in contrast to 73 percent of the eighteen to twenty-four-year-olds, felt that statement was untrue.

One other evidence of the skepticism of age is the response to the statement, "it's not fair to bring children into the world the way things are today." Overall, only 15 percent of the total sample agreed and 77 percent disagreed with that statement.

The bulk of the eighteen to twenty-four-year-old age group (89 percent) disagreed overwhelmingly with that statement. But in the sixty-five and over group, almost one-third (32 percent) agreed, and only slightly more than half (51 percent) disagreed. Obviously, as one ages, one tends to lose the optimism and enthusiasm of youth.

217

One final age-related response pattern was to the statement, "parents often expect too much from their children." Overall, two-thirds of the sample agreed and one-third disagreed with this statement.

However, the greatest agreement (74 percent) is found in the thirty-five to forty-nine-year-olds. That's not really surprising when you realize that these parents are struggling with children who are passing through adolescence into young adulthood. It is during this time when most parents come face to face with youngsters challenging and rebelling against parental wishes.

These parents might be reassured by the responses of the over sixty-five age group to this same statement. They split fifty-fifty on agree/disagree with parents expecting too much. It would seem that both parents and children do mellow with age.

WHY DO WE HATE OUR CHILDREN?

—A seven-year-old boy is referred to welfare authorities after his teachers observe numerous marks on his body. Investigation reveals the child is beaten daily by his mother, because—she says—"He is restless, demands attention all the time, is silly, and just won't learn."

—An eleven-year-old girl is hospitalized because of multiple lacerations and bruises, the result of a severe beating by her stepfather who complains that "the girl is a financial burden."

These are but two instances of the increasingly publicized reality of child abuse in this country. When most of us read of such incidents, we are outraged and incredulous. "How could anyone do that to a child?" We are confident that we don't feel that way about our children. Or do we?

The popular conception of children is that they are lovable, delightful creatures: "living dolls." Children are innocent, wonderful, and charming. How could anybody hate these helpless beings?

If we are honest about our feelings as parents, we know it's really not too hard. For children are also parasites. They are demanding, unprincipled. They do what they want when they want—with no regard for others. They make messes which parents have to clean up—again and again and again and again! They cry. Indeed, often they may cry in spite of our best efforts to make them comfortable and happy, thereby making us feel impotent and frustrated.

They take our time. They suck and drain us. They deplete us. They irritate us. We envy their irresponsibility. And we struggle because we are not supposed to get angry at them; we're supposed to be ever-giving and tolerant of them.

Surely, any parent knows well that children can be exasperating and provocative and trying—to the extreme. To never experience anger in such circumstances is to not be human.

Our children, being our creation, are to some degree a living part of us—an extension of us. Our feelings toward them will, then, reflect some of our feelings toward ourselves. If we have self-doubts, feelings of worthlessness, or a "bad" sense of ourself, we are likely to assume that our child will be similarly bad and perceive our child that way.

This scapegoating is especially likely if the child has some characteristics which set him/her up for it, such as having colic, or some handicap or deficiency.

We can hate our children for a multitude or reasons, not the least of which is that they are going to grow up and displace us. Insofar as we like to have our children be docile, manageable extensions of us, we are upset when they become independent, talk back, or challenge our standards, like letting their hair grow to unconscionable lengths.

One man who has studied child abuse in some depth is Dr. David Gil. He surveyed public attitudes, and found nearly three out of every five respondents (58.3 percent) acknowledged that "almost anybody could at some time injure a child in his care."

Of course, not all of us lose our control with our children—at least not to the degree of child abuse. Yet all of us, if we're honest with ourselves, must recognize our potential for that behavior.

No matter how lovable, there are times for every one of us when it's easy to hate our children!

THE IMPACT OF AN ABNORMAL CHILD

Imagine looking forward with great anticipation to the birth of a baby, only to discover the child has a significant abnormality! Few experiences in life are more painful and unsettling to a mother and father.

The initial reaction of most parents to the discovery of an imperfect newborn child is shock, followed by a period of denial, and then grief. Or there follows a period of soul searching.

The birth of an abnormal child can be a severe blow to one's self-esteem, particularly if the child is your first offspring. You may feel resentment and anger. You wonder why me? Or why us? You may feel recrimination toward your spouse, and then guilt for experiencing such feelings.

It is a stressful experience, which can make or break a marriage. This was the conclusion of a study by Dr. Ann Gath, a British child psychiatrist who followed some families after they gave birth to a defective child.

She studied thirty families into which were born babies with Down Syndrome, the so-called mongolism condition. She compared the adjustment in these families with a comparable group of thirty families into which a normal child had been born. She interviewed these families over a two-year period after the births, and administered a number of questionnaires to assess their adjustment.

She found that mothers of both normal and Down Syndrome babies were prone to depression, changes in mood, and the tendency to feel tired all the time; but the symptoms were slightly more common in the mothers of the abnormal children.

Noted Dr. Gath, "the effect on the mental health of a woman having a baby with mongolism is similar in type and degree to that experienced by other women bringing up small children in difficult circumstances, and not significantly greater than the effect of having a healthy baby."

However, there were some striking differences in the marital relationships of the parents over the period of the study. Sexual dissatisfaction was more common among parents of Down Syndrome babies.

In that group, mothers attributed their sexual problems to a distaste for intercourse after the birth of an imperfect child. Two fathers who complained of impotence said they felt "less of a man" for not producing a normal child.

Further, marital breakdown or severe marital difficulties were found in nearly one-third of the families with an abnormal child. Dr. Gath found no major upheavals in the families which had the normal babies.

Lest one believe that only bad came from the experience of giving birth to a defective child, Dr. Gath found half of the marriages of parents of Down Syndrome children to be "good" marriages, characterized by mutual concern and affection. While overall, the negative measures of marital relationships were higher in the parents of defective children, so were the positive measures also higher in this group.

Despite their grief, the parents of almost half the children in the study felt drawn closer together, and their marriages were strengthened rather than weakened by their shared tragedy.

The strengthening of a marriage by such adversity has also been observed in other studies of parents of children with defects. One study of parents of children with fibrocystic disease found one-half the fathers and nearly two-thirds of the mothers feeling closer to their spouse because of the mutual problems and distress.

Unquestionably, the birth of a child with a defect places a severe strain on a family and tests the strength of the relationship between husband and wife. In such a time of crisis, support from relatives and friends can be most important, and professional counselling may be indicated.

ARE FUNERALS FOR CHILDREN?

The death of a loved one is always a trying time. There is struggle enough to deal with the grief. Yet the immediate family must also come to grips with a host of details which you ordinarily don't think about—including funeral arrangements.

With regard to funerals, one question posed to me is, should the children attend? Is it good for them or bad?

Recently, I came across an excellent discussion of the pros and cons of children attending funerals by Dr. John Schowalter, who is with the Child Study Center in the Department of Pediatrics at the Yale University School of Medicine.

He developed his ideas after being asked to see a number of youngsters who ranged from three to fifteen years of age and who developed symptoms after attending a funeral. Nearly all of the youngsters he saw had openly expressed the wish not to attend the funeral. Those who hadn't admitted later that they didn't want to go but thought it would be improper or "babyish" to say so.

The symptoms which the children developed included trouble falling asleep, fears of becoming ill and dying, fear of going to church. Some had visions at night connected with the funeral service, fearing the return of the dead person whom the child had loved, but who now would take away either the child or the remaining parent(s).

None of the children had previous emotional difficulties, and their adverse reactions developed in an acute manner, either immediately after or within a week of the funeral.

Schowalter acknowledged that many children may attend funerals without developing symptoms, and in the children referred to him, the symptoms often resolved within a month or two without professional help. But nevertheless, those children who did have reactions presented an additional burden to their families at a difficult time.

So how do you determine whether it makes sense for the child to attend the funeral? To find the answer, it is important to know how the child understands death and funerals. Adults can appreciate the concept of death and for them the funeral offers an opportunity for the bereaved to be supported while expressing grief.

The younger child, however, does not grasp the abstract concept of death. Death is more personalized and related to the child's past experience and feelings of guilt, of being good or bad. The child also assumes that others think and feel the same way as he does.

Thus the dead person is still a person, but someone who has gone away, perhaps because of something the child did. Or death may be personified as something or someone who comes and takes the victim and who may return. Such personalized thinking is particularly evident in youngsters between the ages of three and seven or so.

In Schowalter's experience, it is unusual for children under the age of six or seven to experience funerals as a useful event psychologically. He suggests, further, that children around the age of six, seven or eight, be asked if they wish to attend a funeral. "If following the parent's explanation, the child does not wish to go, it is usually sound to respect that decision."

Whether the child goes to the funeral or stays home, the grieving parents may be limited in tuning in to the child's emotional needs. Therefore, a less involved relative or friend may play a useful role in looking after and giving full attention to the youngster.

Another point of note. While it is often helpful to allow a child to see a person who has just died, children are often frightened by the sight of a corpse in an open casket. Noted Schowalter, "The prepared corpse is so artificially 'real' that it seems unreal. Unlike what many morticians suggest, the image seen in an open casket is not what one would wish the child to carry with him. It is not life or death, but a confusing 'fake life' or 'blurred death.'"

Are funerals for children? Not usually.

HOW SHOULD I REACT TO SEX IN CHILDREN?

Dear Dr. Menninger:
I was shocked to find our thirteen-year-old son had tried to get my four-year-old son to practice oral sex on him. I talked to my pediatrician about this, and he seemed to think it was an isolated incident and not to worry. However, he said to keep a close eye on him for any other abnormal behavior.

My problem is that I'm afraid this will happen again, and the little one will not tell me. How can I talk to him if anyone does try this again by scaring him? I'm afraid now that he knows it is not right and that he will be ashamed or scared to tell me.

Yours truly,
Mrs. N. T.

Most adults have difficulty in coming to grips with sexual behavior in children. This may be partly the result of a wish to see children as innocent and without sexual interest; it may also stem from a tendency to attribute to children's sexual activity the same attitudes and motivations of adults.

Both those tendencies are based on false assumptions. Sigmund Freud upset a lot of people in the Victorian era when he pointed out that children are sexual beings. However, the child's

228

view of sex should not be confused as being the same as the adult view of sex.

When an infant is born, the nervous system is not yet mature, particularly the nerves supplying the lower body. This is one reason the infant cannot immediately walk or assert control over bowel and bladder functions. As these nerves do mature, the youngster does become aware of pleasurable sensations in the genital area.

Anyone who observes young children carefully will note they do explore and play with all parts of their body, including the genital area. Often, a child will practice a kind of infantile masturbation.

Most parents misinterpret the thoughts in the child's mind while this occurs. The young child does not really know what adult sex is all about. He or she simply senses a pleasure in the stimulation of that area of the body.

As youngsters grow into elementary school years, they become more aware of other children's bodies and have a natural curiosity to compare one another. Thus, one has the games of "Doctor" and "Nurse." Again, some parents attribute adult sexual interests into this activity of children, although the youngsters at that age still rarely know what adult sex is really about.

Adolescents begin to have more awareness as they mature and attain an adult sexual capacity—physically. However, unless parents have made some effort to educate their children about sexuality, the kids are still likely to be full of misconceptions and misinformation.

The challenge to parents is to avoid panicking when you discover children in one or another form of exploratory sexual play. Sexual behavior of children should not be treated in the same way that you might respond to the same behavior engaged in by two adults.

The best way to keep from frightening your youngster is to approach him matter-of-factly. Share facts about behavior, as well as your attitude about it.

Accept sexual exploration in children as an innocent activity, and do not assume the youngster thinks like you do. You may point out to the child that you don't approve of the behavior, but don't equate "bad" behavior with being totally bad or unacceptable as a person.

TEENAGE SMOKING: "DO AS I SAY, NOT AS I DO"

Dear Dr. Menninger:

My fourteen-year-old daughter, Susan, loves school. The last few weeks of summer, she couldn't wait to get back to classes. She's in the eighth grade in a junior high school where they have been having quite a bit of trouble with teenagers smoking.

This year, the school decided to crack down on the problem, and they have instituted some harsh penalties. The first time a student is caught smoking at school, he or she is given a warning, and the parents are called. The second time, the student is suspended for three days.

Today, I got a call from the principal. He caught Susan smoking, and this was the warning. She says that this was a fluke; she was just taking a drag on a friend's cigarette.

At this point, my wife and I don't know what to do. Even though we both smoke, we don't think that Susan ought to be doing so at her age. I don't know whether to let it pass or to really come down hard on her and bawl her out. What would you suggest?

Sincerely,
D. M.

An increasing number of teenagers are smoking. A national

survey in 1971 found 15 percent of young people smoking.

The latest survey in 1974 reported one out of four (25 percent) young people were now smoking. This compares to a fairly constant report of about 40 percent of adults who smoke (39 percent in 1971, 41 percent in 1974).

Again, the marked increase is in younger age groups. In 1971, only 5 percent of the twelve to thirteen-year-olds were smoking; now that's up to 13 percent. The 1974 survey found 25 percent of the fourteen to fifteen-year-olds were smoking and 38 percent of the sixteen to seventeen-year-olds were smoking. So Susan has a good deal of company.

Since the incidence of smoking in teenagers is so prevalent, I'm not sure you'll get the results you want by either extreme of letting it pass or bawling her out. Rather, I would suggest sitting down and discussing the situation with her in a straightforward manner, touching on the issue of smoking and its relationship to staying in school.

Many times we are faced with rules with which we may disagree. Your daughter and her friends may disagree with the school rules about smoking, but as long as they exist, they are part of her "reality." And she must consider the "cost" of challenging that reality. Is she willing to pay the price of suspension from the school she so enjoys in order to smoke?

Most adolescents think primarily in terms of here and now; they often fail to consider the future consequences of their actions. Your responsibility is to help Susan appreciate those potential consequences, and to then trust her ability to judge the best course of action.

Of course, some teenagers challenge rules as a way to prove they are independent and can do their own thing. The task of the parent is to help the teenagers find a way to do his or her own thing without compromising the future.

In the case of smoking, the future consequences also include the high probability of health problems over the long run, particularly when one starts smoking at an early age and continues it on a regular basis.

However, as long as you and your wife smoke, you present a model with which your daughter may wish to identify. Teenagers do not always appreciate advice of "Do as I say, not as I do."

WHY YOUTH USE DRUGS

What is a teen-ager's motivation to use marijuana? What does it mean?

Two psychiatrists in a court clinic in Massachusetts explored similar questions with a number of adolescents and young adults in trouble because of drug use. They found drug taking was often an attempt at adaptation by a young person, prompted by inner emotional, social and family pressures.

Drs. Stephen Proskauer and Ruick Rolland classified the youngsters they saw into (1) experimental drug users, (2) depressive drug users, and (3) characterological drug users.

The characterological drug users are the smallest group and are more like what most people think of as addicted users. These young people were exposed in early life to deprivation, inconsistency and rejection. They use drugs as a means to cut the pain they experience and are psychologically addicted to the drugs.

The depressive drug users comprise a large number of young people who are seeking an answer to feelings of emptiness, hopelessness, loneliness and worthlessness through drug experiences. Their depressive mood is often not obvious to the casual observer.

Some adolescents in the depressive category appear to be caught in a mutual alienation from their parents. They feel unrelated and unsupported by their parents and increasingly depressed, while the parents react to the youngster's withdrawal as confirming his "badness."

The experimental drug users are perhaps the largest segment of young people. They have taken drugs at one time or another because of one or several reasons—the influence of peer pressure; defiant feelings toward adults or authority; curiosity; desire for a new sensual experience.

Alcohol and tobacco have been used and abused by adolescents for the same reasons for generations. Those substances, too, are often held high in peer group prestige and serve as a means to rebel against parents and authority.

Of note, however, is the finding by Proskauer and Rolland that experimental drug users do not have a compelling need for the drug experience. On the whole, their drug use is casual and intermittent. The young experimenter may openly acknowledge that taking the drug is contrary to "the kind of person I want to be." He may also fully appreciate that the drugs are strongly disapproved by those he loves and respects.

Indeed, the experimental drug user may not have a significant drug problem at all. There is no conclusive evidence of physical, psychological or social damage from casual experimentation; and scientific data do not indicate that use of marijuana must automatically lead to the use of "harder" drugs and delinquency.

Actually, Proskauer and Rolland observe that the very process of labelling an experimenter as a confirmed drug abuser, and subjecting him to overly strong legal or disciplinary action or rejection, may confirm a fear within him: "Maybe I really am that bad." This may prompt continued drug use, fulfilling the prophecy of family and community.

The approach to handling the drug user depends upon the category of user. For the experimental user, the best approach may be deliberate noninterference, informal counselling and an educational program. Treated with understanding or just left to himself, the experimenter may just drop out of the drug scene in due time, none the worse, and possibly even better because of the experience.

Depressive drug users can benefit from various types of psychotherapy and goal-oriented activity group programs with peers. The characterological drug user often requires a residential treatment program directed to meet the needs of addicted individuals.

WHY TEENAGERS GET PREGNANT

"Why? Why did it happen? I thought she knew better!"

That was one parent's reaction upon the discovery of the pregnancy of a teenage daughter. The question was almost rhetorical, with no expectation of an answer. And usually there is no simple answer, but there are reasons why.

Dr. Sherry Hatcher, psychologist at the University of Michigan Health Service, studied a group of pregnant teenagers to find some of the reasons. She found different motivations and meanings for girls at different stages of adolescent development —early, middle and late.

The early adolescent girl has little or distorted information about matters of conceptions and contraception. She tends to disavow any and all responsibility for becoming pregnant, blaming it either on a little-known boy or perhaps on her mother for failing to provide adequate sex education.

The motivation for the early adolescent's pregnancy seems to reflect a complex relationship with her own mother, with a wish both to break away from her and at the same time become more dependent upon her. Usually she is still too tied to her mother to actually conceive of herself as a mother. A secondary motivation for the pregnancy seems to be a testing of her new and mysterious body functions as a woman.

The middle adolescent girl, unlike the early adolescent, appears to have sufficient understanding of the process to avoid becoming pregnant. But she fails to protect herself and invariably blames someone else for her plight, often an authority figure —doctor, boyfriend, even her father.

Hatcher found that the girl in middle adolescence who became pregnant seemed to wish to have a baby for or by (in fantasy) her father. The experience of pregnancy centered around a competitive fantasy that she can do whatever mother can. She may also wish to prove independence through the pregnancy, but is ambivalent and still too dependent upon her parents to break away in a less rebellious manner.

Motherhood is idealized by the middle adolescent girl, but the feelings are changeable, sometimes a romantic view of maternal bliss, sometimes a shuddering at the thought of caring for an infant. She is, nevertheless, supremely conscious of her pregnant state, in contrast to the early adolescent who tends to deny being pregnant.

Late adolescents seem to know all about conception and contraception. They are generally aware that the pregnancy is their responsibility, the result of a conscious or unconscious slip, such as forgetting to take the pill. Still, a number of these girls are critical of their parents for inadequate sex education.

When a late adolescent girl finds herself pregnant, she is rarely surprised. In some way, she senses an unconscious planning of the pregnancy. Most often, she acknowledges the possibility that her conception was motivated by a wish to get her boyfriend to propose marriage and make a permanent commitment to her.

This motivation to obtain increased affection and a commitment from her boyfriend is in sharp contrast to the early and middle adolescent girls. For them the boyfriend is largely irrelevant and the pregnancy may signal the end to the relationship.

Most late adolescent girls view pregnancy as a joyous event under the right circumstances. Being unmarried and pregnant, they are filled with understandable anxieties and guilt. However, they tend to deal with the physical and emotional aspects of pregnancy more realistically than do the younger girls.

The older girls show the beginnings of a genuine wish to love and care for a child. They have less ambivalence about seeing themselves as mothers, and have worked through more of the early childhood conflicts that are evident in the younger adolescents.

WITH THE LOSS OF A SON . . .

Dear Dr. Menninger:

I have just read your article on "How Do You Face Death?" Well, I just wanted to let you know that I faced it a few weeks ago. My son would have been seventeen this month.

I don't know how other parents face this. I am just going crazy. It is just awful to have a kid all those years, get him almost grown, and then lose him.

I feel sorry for anyone who has lost a child. Now I know how it is. I have talked to a priest, but that didn't help. Now I don't know what to do.

I can't sleep much or eat properly.

I have two other kids—one fourteen and one fifteen. And I can't have any more. I am thirty-four-years-old. I feel at this time that I will never be truly happy since I lost my child.

Can you please tell me what to do about all this. I don't know what to do next to keep my mind.

From a sad mother.
D. H.

A letter like your always leaves me at a loss for words, because the pain resonates within me. What can anyone say to relieve your pain? No much, really. Any more than talking to someone who is badly hurt takes away their pain.

You have become a member in a special club—parents who have lost a child. My wife and I are members, though our loss was an infant son. But we found in the time of our grief that there were many others around us who had a similar experience. And they shared how they gradually came to grips with the loss and again found happiness.

It is awful to lose a child after investing so much of yourself in raising him. To have him suddenly taken just as he is approaching adulthood seems grossly unfair. The pain may be increased because of the particular place your first-born has in your heart as the child who taught you how to be a parent.

Is it really better to have loved and lost than never to have loved at all? You have to answer that question now. And, I hope, you will be able to recall enough of the pleasures in your life and his that made the experience of raising him worth it.

Depression is the result of feelings about a loss which cannot be easily expressed—feelings of resentment and anger which are turned inwardly. Thus you feel down in the dumps, discouraged, hopeless, unhappy. And you have trouble sleeping and don't have any appetite.

What's to be done? First, accept the fact that you have been injured seriously, much the same as if you experienced an amputation. A part of you has been ripped away. After such an injury, you must allow some time for healing. This, too, shall pass.

While you did not feel talking to the priest helped, you may yet find some help in talking to someone else. Especially helpful may be sharing your feelings with someone who has gone through the same experience, a fellow member of the "club." You can discover you are not so alone in this kind of experience.

Often it is helpful to get involved in some activity which keeps you busy. Clean the house from stem to stern. Physical activity and hard work can provide an outlet for angry feelings which may be bottled up by the depression.

Beware of ruminations of guilt or feelings that you somehow did not do all the things you should have done for your son.

If you have a religious commitment, you may find your faith is an important sustaining force. Death is never easy to deal with because it seems beyond any reason to explain. Faith in a Higher Power overlooking our earthly lives can be reassuring.

Finally, keep your life in perspective. You have two other children. Give them the opportunity to help you find happiness again. While your nest may be suddenly "one-third" empty, it is still two-thirds full.

PART FOUR

Coping

A number of years ago, I came across a cartoon of a nurse tending to newborns in a hospital nursery. Prominently displayed on the wall of the nursery was a sign: "Caution: Living is Hazardous to Your Health." Presumably, you have gotten the message by now that a successful adaptation in life requires a realistic perception of those hazards and an assumption of personal responsibility for what happens to you.

You can cop-out by saying that you didn't choose to come into this world, it was someone else's idea. Conceived by others, most of us are shoved into the cold, cruel world with force and intensity at birth. While we may be protected and cared for in infancy and childhood, we can't escape disappointments. Eventually, we must face the fact that our parents have their imperfections. They too have "feet of clay." Nonetheless, we may be reluctant to give up hopes for a godfather or good fairy who will come to our rescue and solve our problems, making right all the injustices in our world. As one of my patients was approaching the completion of several years of psychoanalysis, he reported he was ready for termination because he could now accept the fact that "life just isn't fair!" He didn't like it, but he could accept it. That's the way things are, and there's not too much you can really do about it.

One of my colleagues admitted that it took him nearly a half-century before he finally realized that life is a "do-it-yourself-thing," and you have to assume responsibility for yourself. That doesn't mean you can't create some godfathers or good fairies in your life to help make things easier, finding friends and companions who will help and support you when you are down.

When you can acknowledge that life is full of injustice and there aren't any simple solutions to all the hurts one experiences, you're on the right track. Of course, there are still many people who are sure they have found *the* solution—Laetrile, love, lots of love, religion, self-help books. The search for Nirvana or the bluebird of happiness is pursued relentlessly, as if it is to be found just around the next corner. Or else the pains and tensions of life are blotted out by diazepam (Valium)—"Mother's Little Helper"—or a six-pack of beer and several highballs.

Sometimes, in search for guidelines in life, people fall back on witty sayings or proverbs. Such aphorisms can be absurd when you try to apply them all at once. I recall one such grouping hanging on the wall in the office of my favorite medical school teacher: "Keep your eye on the ball. Keep your ear to the ground. Keep your nose to the grindstone. Now, try and work that way!"

Nevertheless, there are many useful concepts for living found in aphorisms which may help you make the best of the life you are in, rather than your persisting in a fruitless search for the perfect existence. One such observation often quoted by that same medical school professor, Dr. Felix Wroblewski, was that it's far more important in life to like what you do than to do what you like. He was a living example of that observation. He had not originally wanted to go into medicine. He had wanted to be like his father, a chemist. But his father insisted he go to medical school. So he did, most reluctantly, hating it all the way. Only after he was drafted into the Army and given responsibility for general medical care for some soldiers and their dependents at a camp in New Jersey did he find enjoyment in the practice of medicine. Subsequently, even though he had an institutional job and was teaching medical students techniques of physical diagnosis, he continued to carry on a small private practice as a family physician. Further, he found a way to satisfy his initial desires by joining a colleague in research which combined chemistry and medicine. This work culminated in the identification of one of the first diagnostic blood tests for a specific enzyme which is released into the blood stream from damaged heart muscle at the time of a heart attack.

When you're down and out and have been taken advantage of by someone else, it may be hard to see anything positive. You're much more aware of the half-empty part of the glass than the half-full part. Yet, I am increasingly struck by the potential for good to be found in everyone. Of course, bad exists; but, given the option, the vast majority of people respond positively to the opportunity to be good. They want a positive and constructive identity, to be seen as persons who leave life a better place because of their presence. When I worked in a federal reformatory, I found most of the correctional officers didn't really want to be seen as "punishing" people. They preferred to be seen as persons who were oriented toward helping incarcerated offenders become good citizens.

Most people split the world into "good" and "bad." Sometimes the split is quite interesting. Surveys of attitudes of the public toward the medical profession have found doctors in general to be considered greedy, status-conscious, interested only in making a lot of money. But when asked about their personal physician, the overwhelming response is positive—he's a hard working, conscientious practitioner who is highly respeced. The same litany may be heard about lawyers or policemen or politicians or most any profession. The group as a whole is vested with negative attributes, but the ones we know personally are good guys. Of course, every profession has its superior practitioners and its bummers. And similarly, each person has moments when he may sway from a commitment to perfection and idealism and the Golden Rule to a more self-centered orientation.

If you are to come to grips with the hazards in life, you do have to know and respect yourself. This means accepting both the good and the bad within oneself, rather than assuming one is all good and attributing the bad to others. Everyone experiences unacceptable thoughts and feelings. I have never had a patient who has not at some point confessed the fear that if he really told me everything, I probably wouldn't have a thing further to do with him. Having bad thoughts or feelings is not the important point; it's what you do about them. It has been frequently observed that you're not responsible for having feelings, but you are responsible for what you do with them. Thus, President-elect Jimmy Carter could acknowledge in a *Playboy* interview that he had experienced lustful feelings. But it's clear that he knew the difference between having feelings and acting on them.

There are a number of principles to keep in mind while grappling with and adjusting to the many hazards in life: Acknowledge the potential for good in people, while respecting the presence of badness. Respect and accept the presence of feelings, while not being compelled to act on them. Learn the restorative and cleansing value of giving of oneself. Develop skills to turn change to your advantage, focussing on the new challenges rather than dwelling on the losses.

These principles are illustrated in different ways in the ensuing

248

essays. Meanwhile, when you can accept the fact that life is just not fair and can proceed on your way without being filled with bitterness or preoccupied with a sense of injustice, you will have achieved no small accomplishment. You are well on the way toward the ultimate ideal of emotional maturity, the criteria for which were formulated by my father, Dr. William C. Menninger:

Having the ability to deal constructively with reality.

Having the capacity to adapt to change.

Having a relative freedom from symptoms that are produced by tensions and anxieties.

Having the capacity to find more satisfaction in giving than receiving.

Having the capacity to relate to other people in a consistent manner with mutual satisfaction and helpfulness.

Having the capacity to sublimate, to direct one's instinctive hostile energy into creative and constructive outlets.

Having the capacity to love.

AN EXCUSE IN ADVANCE

Who hasn't, at one time or another, come to the end of a day with the knowledge that you had to have something done by the morning, but you just didn't have the time to get it done?

You worry about what is going to happen because you haven't gotten the job or the assignment done. You kick yourself for putting it off until there was not enough time left to do it. You dream up all sorts of excuses to explain why you didn't get it done.

All who have had that experience will appreciate why two of our youngsters are still talking about a Valentine they received this year—a greeting from their teachers that they hadn't expected.

It was a mimeographed sheet, with a big red heart outlined in the center, and a message:

Be My Valentine
This Valentine is a coupon
which can be used as a
subsitute for one daily
assignment.

In addition, there was some small print at the bottom—which you might have expected:

Notice: Void Where Prohibited
(Long range assignments and tests)

250

That was the limitation put on by David's teacher, Miss Cathy Gallagher. Will's teacher, Mrs. Shirley Montague, indicated that the coupon was good only during February. Even so, you'd better believe that along with a third colleague who also distributed coupons, Mrs. Ann Perry, those teacher really scored with their pupils that day.

Needless to say, the kids have put their "coupons" in a safe place, much like the Monopoly player who gets a "Get Out of Jail Free" card from Chance or Community Chest. It's such a nice feeling to have that insurance against being caught short... at least once.

Mrs. Montague first started the practice several years ago, when she read about the idea in a teacher's magazine. It was presented as something to make kids happy. But she found it can be a valuable learning experience for the kids.

Most of the children don't cash in their coupons right away. They hang onto it, saving it for the "biggest" assignment that comes along. Indeed, some save it so long that Mrs. Montague's expiration date passes without their realizing it. And some never do attempt to use it.

Other kids pick up immediately on the opportunity and play it for all it's worth. Mrs. Montague ran out of her original supply this year and had to prepare a new coupon. She forgot to write in the test exclusion, and one of her pupils immediately wanted to apply it to an upcoming math test. He didn't get to.

The coupon is a small token with considerable positive psychological impact. Like insurance, it is an anxiety reliever. It is an assurance of being acceptable even if you are not always perfect.

The reality is that one missed assignment by a student is unlikely to have a deterrent effect on learning over the long haul. To be forgiven in advance for one missed assignment can free the student to progress without getting hung up in a struggle with the teacher. That positive experience can spill over to other areas.

The coupon is also a concrete token of "caring." While these teachers took advantage of February 14 as a day of caring, you don't have to be restricted to that date. A host of occasions might be used for the same purpose.

WHO SAID YOU CAN'T TRUST CAB DRIVERS?

The conversation during the evening ranged far and wide. Almost all of it had to with one or another kind of wrong-doing:

—Physicians ripping off the government by adding big laboratory service markups to bills submitted to medicare and medicaid;

—An "alleged" doctor arrested after complaints that he sexually abused unknowing, hypnotized patients;

—The congressional sex scandals—both putting women on the payroll primarily for sexual services, and being on the make with police-"prostitutes."

The inevitable question: Who can you trust?

Several weeks ago, I came across a marvelous treatise on this subject: Steven Brill's account of "A New York Cabby Story You Won't Believe" in *New York* magazine.

Brill had the same feeling about the New York taxi drivers "that most people have about politicians, that they're all crooks." In advance of the major conventions in the Big Apple this summer, Brill made his own test of the cabbies' trustworthiness.

He posed as a foreigner with no knowledge of English and no idea of where he was going. He got into a dozen licensed Yellow Cabs around the city to see how many cheated him.

Before beginning his experiment, he polled some friends for their predictions of the outcome. The majority thought three-fourths of the cabbies would be crooks. Only one friend, the least cynical, predicted as few as two would fleece him.

His "startling" findings: With two relatively petty exceptions, each driver was completely honest. "So honest," he reported, "that this became a story about decency in New York and a good lesson for bigots of any persuasion." Indeed, two additional drivers he approached to take him to a place only a block away refused to take him, advising he walk.

In all, he took twelve cabs and spent about thirty-five dollars. Every driver took the most direct route. Two of the twelve beat him out of a total of $1.50. Noted Brill, "These two did cheat, but only after I almost begged them to."

Counting the two who refused to take him a block—one even got out of his cab and walked ten feet to point the way, assuring him he could walk there faster—twelve of fourteen taxi drivers he approached were completely honest even in the face of extreme temptation.

These honest twelve cabbies appeared to Brill to represent a reasonable cross-section of New York, based on names, looks and accents.

The fascinating irony was cab driver Donald Campbell's admonition to Brill as he let him off. Be wary, "everyone in New York is out to rob you." That is the prevailing myth, not only in New York. Yet the lesson Brill learned is something to be shared more widely.

The potential for good and evil lies within everyone. In the face of temptation, there are those who will be turned to a selfish, exploitative course of action. The evidence suggests, however, that you can trust more people than you think, that most people in gainful, legitimate employment will be worthy of your trust.

You will continue to read news stories of corrupt politicians, or policemen who go wrong, or fraudulent doctors. But don't be misled by these reported incidents. They are news because they are exceptions. Most people are like you and me—we really want to do a good job at what we are doing and get respect and a fair return for our honest labor.

FLOWER POWER

"Dad, why don't you write something about flowers?"

That was my son Fritz, who at age twenty has been much impressed with the impact of flowers. Not just flowers in the garden, nor flowers associated with the "flower childen"; but flowers as gifts to others.

He's had a number of experiences giving flowers. As a youngster, he would celebrate the first day of May by putting a basket of posies on the doorknob of the neighbors, ring the doorbell, run off to hide and see the reaction when the door was opened.

At age sixteen, as a junior in high school, Fritz gave that old May Day practice a new twist. He took some birthday money and bought two dozen roses. He took them to school; and during the day, he passed them out.

The recipients: a couple of teachers; two fellows, for their girl friends; some close friends; some passing acquaintances. And he had a wonderful time enjoying people's reactions.

The next year he did the same thing. During the day, several people asked him if he had some of the roses for sale, but he kept them just to give away—some planned ahead, some just on impulse. Still having one at the end of the day, he impulsively gave it to a casual acquaintance, a girl with whom he had worked on the student-faculty board.

That impulsive action had an unexpected dividend. Later that evening, Fritz suddenly realized that he didn't have his backpack, with all his books and papers contained therein. He couldn't remember where he had left it.

The doorbell rang, and the young lady to whom he had impulsively given the last rose was at the door—with his backpack. He had left it downtown after an after-school activity. She had noticed it and picked it up to return it to him.

When he went off to college, he sent flowers to others by mail. The rewards there included a long distance acquaintance with one young lady who wrote him after her roommates (whom he knew) got flowers, and she didn't. He got to know her better, and in due course, she got some too.

This summer, he became aware of a friend who was most unhappy. Her parents were splitting, and she realized that she didn't have the relationship she wants with either of her parents. An only child, she felt lost and alone.

Her distress evoked a reaction of sympathy, but Fritz knew there was little he could do to help. So he took her some flowers. She was pleased and appreciative of his concern. But Fritz acknowledges that "I also did it for me. For some reason, it just made me feel better to send them."

Why do flowers have such an impact? Most likely because the flower symbolizes feelings. It is an action message, an articulation of emotion which says more than words.

Traditionally, flowers have come to represent a sense of caring for someone—someone celebrating an anniversary or a special holiday; someone ill, in the hospital; someone bereaved at the loss of a loved one. Received unexpectedly, this token of caring can have an even greater impact.

The tradition of giving flowers goes back a long way. Why does the flower get used in this way? Perhaps because it represents a special beauty—and often fragrance too—in life, a natural piece of art.

The flower is nature's creativity at one of its peaks. And by association with the beauty of the flower, both the giver and the receiver become more beautiful. The radiance of the flower can thereby obscure some of the ugliness and discomfort in life.

A DAY OF LOVE

It's most unlikely that you've ever heard of Ted Walters. He's a caring individual who operates quietly and sensitively and effectively as an elementary school principal in Topeka, Kansas.

If you're like most parents, you tend to take for granted the impact on your children's life by a Ted Walters or the teachers who teach in his school. Of course, at the time of the school's "open house," or in teacher conferences, you may get briefly acquainted.

But about the only time there is any special recognition of a teacher or a principal is when they are leaving, by retirement or assignment to another school. One year, as the school year was coming to a close, the PTA executive committee at Randolph Elementary, where Ted was principal, was planning the usual reception for retiring teachers. Then someone said, why don't we do something now to say thanks to Ted Walters?

The question was how he could be thanked in some different way. The answer was provided by an earlier experience which several parents had with custom-stenciled T-shirts.

So a project was conceived. With the help of an art instructor, a stencil was designed. Room mothers quietly contacted each parent to obtain a T-shirt, old or new, for each child. Several mothers spent a couple of evenings stenciling the collected shirts, and they were returned to each child's home. In due course, the whole school was in on the secret—parents, children, teachers, custodian, secretary, even the principal's wife—and nobody spilled the beans.

The principal regularly greeted the children each day as they entered the school. So on "T-Day," a cooperative district administrator scheduled an early morning conference at the district office. And all the children wore their T-shirts to school; only a couple forgot, and there were extras in the office to cover that.

When all was ready, a call was made downtown requesting the principal report back to the school. On his way, he worried about what terrible thing might have happened to prompt his being called. He was sure it must something awful when, as he approached the school, he heard the bell (which the custodian rang to signal the children and teachers to assemble).

As he entered the school and was ushered to the multipurpose room, he was greeted by a sea of T-shirts proclaiming "Randolph Kids Love Ted Walters"—the "love" was in the shape of a heart —and a chorus of "For He's a Jolly Good Fellow!"

Ted Walters is a stocky fellow who is rarely at a loss for words. But he was speechless this time, absolutely devastated with the loving appreciation of the assembled school. And the joyous exuberance of all the participants in such unabashed affection was glorious. I doubt that I shall ever witness an event with such impact on everybody who participated.

Sure, there have been many variations of days of appreciation. And they are almost always heart-rending. Best known are the "days" for a sports hero or a returning war hero, honored by an assembled multitude.

But there's something special added when it is completely unexpected. Especially when it's a tribute to an unsung hero like Ted Walters, a deserving, beautiful human being who represents every man and woman committed to earnestly and effectively educating our children.

The "gift" to Ted was a red T-shirt with the stenciled message. (His wife was given one which had added, "Me too.") And that gift continues to be pinned on the wall of his office. Not only did he feel good all that day as he saw every child wearing that message of love, so did we, because we all felt that special joy of loving!

THE VALUE OF GIVING

Giving and taking are basic activities in which we engage throughout life. We enter this world without the real capacity to give anything to others in any meaningful way. Our earliest months are spent entirely in taking.

In our infancy, we could not survive if someone did not look out for us and provide our basic needs for food, shelter and love. The infant expects to be taken care of, and it's a rude awakening to discover that others will not always automatically meet our needs.

So we have to find ways to get those things we need for survival. And early in childhood, we learn that one way to get what we want is to earn it—by good behavior, by giving something to others, especially our parents. We search for some balance between just taking from others what we want, and behaving in a way that gets them to reward us.

In my professional life, I have had the unusual opportunity to work with people who have been primarily "takers"—criminal offenders sentenced to prison—and people who have been dedicated to giving of themselves—Peace Corps and VISTA volunteers.

In addition, in clinical work with patients, I have seen many people who were so restricted and self-limited that they could find no satisfaction in giving. And I have seen the remarkable transformation of these people as they begin to be able to give and grow.

It is exciting to observe a person who has never felt secure enough to invest outside himself, begin to try it. As he does so, you can see him envision new horizons and find satisfactions never before achieved.

The ultimate of this experience is the security and contentment of people who have found themselves while giving to others. Few experiences in my life have been quite as impressive as meeting with a group of Peace Corps volunteers overseas in a completion of service conference and hearing them describe the new perspective on life resulting from their service.

In recent years, I have also been struck by the shift in my children at Christmas. As they mature, it is obvious that their greatest satisfaction shifts from the pleasure of opening their own gifts, to the pleasure in seeing their brothers and sisters open the gifts they have given one another.

Our society places much emphasis on duties and obligations. In so many ways, it seems people must be coerced to give to charity, the United Way, or to give of themselves in voluntary service. Perhaps that is a function of our human motivation for self-satisfaction.

A basic principle of economics is that careful investment and reinvestment of capital is a key stimulus to the growth of an economy and at the same time the best way to make money. This is in contrast to the stagnation which occurs when you just put your money in a sock. This principle is no less true for one's emotional investments in life.

One may dwell upon the Golden Rule—doing unto others as you would have them do unto you—because this is the "right" or "good" way to be. Actually, it is the most effective way to be assured that you will, in return, be treated in that way by others.

How often it is that the people who receive the most love from others are those people who have much of it to give; and their giving of love, of themselves, seems always to be returned with dividends.

My father, the late Dr. Will Menninger, listed a number of attributes as criteria for emotional maturity, and one of the most important of these is the capacity to find more satisfaction in giving than receiving.

Yet, the true value of giving is expressed in a Nigerian proverb which I first became aware of through the Peace Corps—and it is my favorite: "When the right hand washes the left hand, the right hand becomes clean also."

THE ANNUAL MADNESS OF THE WORLD
SERIES . . . A FANTASTIC HIGH

Fall is upon us. And with it comes the annual madness of baseball's playoffs and World Series, and the weekend football mania.

While these two sports dominate the newspaper sports pages and television screens in this country, it's clear that sports events excite a great deal of interest and attention all over the world.

Why? How is it that the actions of nine men on a baseball field, plus some teammates, can so prompt people to become glued to the radio or television to follow their exploits? (More than once, I've had the radio on while batting out a column, keeping tabs of the latest scores.)

What is it about the activity of a football team that will immobilize an incredible number of able-bodied, hale and hearty men on successive Sunday afternoons, much to the chagrin and irritation of their wives?

For the athletes, sports present an obvious route to fame and fortune, as well as to personal accomplishment. But what for the spectators? Why do people shell out such sums of money to watch others perform?

Obviously, spectating must gratify some powerful emotional needs, for one would be hard put to label such mania as rational. Consider those two senior citizens who have never missed a Dodger game since the team moved to Los Angeles.

As a child, I recall identifying with the exploits of sports heroes and daydreaming of having the ability to be so accomplished and so acclaimed. In high school and college, athletics served as a symbol of being part of something larger than oneself.

In childhood, you are constantly reminded of your small size and relative insignificance in the world. You wish for the power and ability to be significant. One way to get that power is to join with a more powerful person or group of persons.

Even if you don't have the passing arm of Joe Namath in his prime, or the consistency and coordination of Rod Carew in hitting baseballs, you can vicariously thrill in their accomplishments and feel better because of their success.

Spectating offers more than identification with success and achievement. It provides an escape from life's humdrum. It is a "timeout" from everyday responsibilities. Further, it also is an activity with a license for emotional release.

In the stadium, you can freely express your feelings and scream epithets at the umpire or the opposition or the failings of your favorites. If your team wins, you can have a fantastic "high" without the aid of booze or pot or any other stimulant.

Few emotional experiences in my life match the exhilaration of being part of the Stanford student body rooting section in the heat of a big game with California, screaming in unison at the critical moment. The yell: "Give 'em . . . the Axe, the Axe, the Axe. Right in . . . the neck, the neck, the neck!"

In Dorcas Susan Butt's book, *Psychology of Sport,* she observes that "outlets for emotional expression and frustration are few, and sport offers such an outlet to many people. Sport draws people together in a communion that is bizarre and unnatural.

"Sport draws people together to witness, identify and partici-

266

pate in a contest where the predominant perception is of people struggling against one another . . . a struggle for superiority in which there is a victor and a vanquished."

The repeated efforts of a child to master difficult situations are thus also played out in athletic contests.

While the child within us may aspire to the omnipotence of Superman, or Wonder Woman, the reality is that we all have our limitations. If, momentarily, we can escape the bonds of our reality and live vicariously in the superb achievements of the successful athlete or championship team, what's wrong with that?

WARM HANDS, WARM HEARTS

The old saying goes, "cold hands, warm heart." But let me share with you one instance where warm hands prompted warm hearts. It is also another illustration of the satisfaction to be found in helping one another.

Several years ago, a group of parents of disadvantaged children went before the local board of education to ask for money. They wanted some federal funds for the education of the disadvantaged to be spent on mittens, to protect the little hands during winter of youngsters in the preschool Head Start and elementary school Follow-Through programs.

At the time, my wife, Connie, was a member of the board. As a mother, she recognized the need for mittens. But she felt there must be other resources in the community to meet this need without using tax dollars. Besides, the federal guidelines did not permit spending Title I money this way.

Connie likes to knit, and she knows accomplished knitters can knit almost automatically while watching or listening to something else. She herself has long used knitting to keep her hands occupied on long drives or during meetings, even board of education meetings on occasion. She was sure there were many others who enjoyed knitting and who would love the opportunity to be a part of something like this.

With the help of a local newspaper columnist, Connie spread

the word. She offered to provide a mitten pattern and yarn to anyone willing to knit mittens; and she accepted donations from people to buy yarn. The response was remarkable.

A host of retired women, long-time knitters, called for yarn. Several nursing homes made it a project for their residents, as did the retired teachers association. The activity therapy department of the state hospital added mitten knitting to their fall activity projects.

The local Campfire girls set up a "Turkey Tree" in a cooperative local department store to be "feathered" with mittens for the Head Start youngsters. At first, many of the girls just bought mittens to put on the tree, but more recently the older women have been teaching the young ones how to knit.

The result of this on-going project has been a steady supply of mittens for needy youngsters ever since. But the by-products of the project are no less impressive. Older women who felt put out to pasture found a new way to be involved in a useful and needed activity. They were delighted to turn an old, enjoyable skill to such beneficial use. And they benefited as much as the children.

One elderly woman who made fifty pair watching television said it made her feel good because not all that time was wasted. A retired policeman's wife turned out over one hundred pair. And all the women reported feeling an inner warmth as they kept their fingers busy.

In addition, the project has expanded the horizons of many of the retired women. With new "grandparent-grandchild" relationships, several of the nursing homes have adopted school classes for other special projects.

And the knitters are not the only ones who feel good, as indicated by one letter my wife received:

"Dear Mrs. Menninger: It's 'Mitten Time' again, isn't it? And I want to be a part of this most beautiful project. Hope this love gift will buy a skein or two of yarn for your dedicated knitters. Wish you loads of success, and God Bless You Always."

IF YOU'RE THINKING OF MOVING

Dear Dr. Menninger:

My husband has a good job and we have been happy in our present home for ten years. We have three children, all now in elementary school. Now my husband has an opportunity to get a better job, but it requires moving to another state. We wonder how our children may be affected by the move. Do you have any suggestions about what we should do?

Sincerely,
S. R.

Census figures make it clear that a large portion of our population moves each year. Moving can be an exciting adventure which opens new vistas, and it can be an awesome and depressing task. Such a profound change is always unsettling, and there are things you can do to make it easier.

One of my colleagues, Dr. Jorge de la Torre, moved his family this past summer to Houston, Texas, where he accepted a position with the Baylor University Medical Center. On a visit there this fall, we talked about the things you should consider in moving.

The first, critical step is making the decision. Husband and wife should carefully think through the advantages and disadvantages of a move. It is important for you to make a clear and firm decision about the best thing to do.

In making your decision, you should have as thorough an assessment of the new situation as possible. What does it offer your husband in his life career? What does it offer you and the children as individuals? What does it offer the family as a whole? The most exciting job in the world is not much good if the rest of the family is miserable.

Ideally, both husband and wife should have the opportunity to visit the new community in advance of any move. Give yourself time to become familiar with the different elements in the new community, so you can find a place to live which is compatible with your own interests and activities.

Visit different neighborhoods, churches, community resources, schools. (How to assess a school is an important task in itself.)

Generally, once parents feel comfortable and settled with a decision to move, the children will pick up that attitude and be reassured. And they will most likely respond accordingly. They also will appreciate and profit from a chance to help plan for the move.

In some families, the husband is an employee of a corporation or organization which orders a move. There is a difference between making a move entirely of your own choosing and one which you reluctantly accept as an order or as the only route to a promotion.

Children will sense if you have mixed feelings about moving. In such a case, both you and they are likely to have a more difficult adjustment. Actually, every move involves some negative feelings, some losses, which you should anticipate. The more you can deal with those feelings openly, the better it will be for you and the children. Don't try to pretend all is perfect if it is not.

When the time arrives for the move, allow the children some time to adjust. If possible, the husband should schedule some extra time with the family. The loss of the children's playmates left behind may be compensated for by increased family closeness and activity.

In the first weeks in the new community, allow more time on weekends and after hours for the family to do things together. Gradually expand the horizons of the children to the new community, giving them time to pull together and organize their impressions of their new life setting. And tolerate some grief for friends left behind in the former community.

MESSAGE FOR A NEW YEAR

Dear Reader:

Happy New Year!

Beyond this greeting, may I take this opportunity to share some thoughts to be kept in mind in these rapidly changing times. It is ironical that in these days of incredible technological development designed to make life so much easier, that that change can be so unsettling.

In his book, *Future Shock,* Alvin Toffler described symptoms of the "disease of change." However you label the condition, there are real stresses on people facing frequent change. In coping with these stresses, let me suggest some guidelines.

1. Keep a touch of humility and acknowledge your limitations. Although there are those people who always put themselves down, if you're like most, you tend to think you are better than others. In doing this, you are likely to deny your limits and think you really can do anything you put your mind to.

Unfortunately, that is not true. We all have our limits, and that includes you. Everyone has a breaking point; under sufficient stress, you can break down physically or emotionally. I have never found a more graphic representation of this point that in the opening paragraphs of Dr. Karl Menninger's first book, *The Human Mind,* first published in 1930. He put it this way:

"When a trout rising to a fly gets hooked on a line and finds

274

itself unable to swim about freely, it begins a fight which results in struggles and splashes and sometimes an escape. Often, of course, the situation is too tough for him.

"In the same way the human being struggles with his environment and with the hooks that catch him. Sometimes he masters his difficulties; sometimes they are too much for him. His struggles are all that the world sees, and it usually misunderstands them. It is hard for a free fish to understand what is happening to a hooked one.

"Sooner or later, however, most of us get hooked. How much of a fight we have on our hands then depends upon the hook, and, of course, on us. If the struggle gets too violent, if it throws us out of the water, if we run afoul of other strugglers, we become 'cases' in need of help and understanding."

All too often, when you do get hooked, you want to fix the blame on someone else for what has gone wrong. While that may be true to some extent, more often the wiser course is to explore your own contribution to your problems.

2. Recognize the power of expectations and be alert to the potential of the self-fulfilling prophecy. You may have contributed to your problem unwittingly—it happens all the time. You affect other's reactions to you by how you approach them—by your body posture, your facial expression, your tone of voice, your choice of language—all conveyed so subtly that you don't realize what you are doing.

3. Avoid getting fixed into an extreme position which alienates you from other people. In recent years, there has been much polarization of people to one or another side of an issue, resulting in an attitude that "you're either with me or against me."

Differences are inevitable in this world, as are frictions between people. But if we are to survive all together, we are going to have to focus more on things we have in common. We will have to agree to disagree without losing respect for one another.

4. Learn to listen carefully to others. That's a rare capacity—to listen. More often than not, you enter a conversation filled with your own concerns and unable to appreciate where others are coming from. Listening in its fullest sense requires empathy, the ability to sense another person's feelings, hopes, fears.

5. Finally, respect that it may be far more important in life to like what you do, than to do what you like. That was the advice of my favorite medical school professor, and if makes sense. The pastures in the distance look greener only because the height of the grass across the way conceals the bare spots on the ground which are so obvious on the ground at your feet.

THE MAGIC WORDS

In childhood, I was often told that the two most important words in the English language are "Thank You." Every year, when we celebrate Thanksgiving, I am reminded of the impact of those words.

They are simple words, and they shouldn't be so hard to say. Yet how often it is that people fail to say them. Many times, it matters not that they go unsaid—but they can be very important. And they can have a remarkable impact when they are recived unexpectedly. It is always a shot in the arm to learn that someone has noticed and cares about what you are doing. Such a thank you may be like frosting on a cake, or even more.

Several years ago, as director of a clinical section of the local state hospital, I was aware of the enormous hours of time spent by volunteers working in the hospital. They came to arrange for social activities for patients, to escort patients on shopping trips, to work with them in shops, to help the staff with tasks of filing, and do so many other things. All too often the regular staff tended to take their efforts for granted.

I knew these people weren't volunteering just to get somebody's thanks. They did it because it made them feel good to be of service and to give time and concern to others who needed it. They did appreciate the annual ceremony of recognition for their hours which was held each spring. But I thought Thanksgiving was time to thank them again, and sent each one a note to again say thank you. And the positive reactions which I received were striking, in large part because the additional thanks were so unexpected.

We don't start out life with any great motivation to give to or thank others. The infant and young child are motivated primarily to get "what I want when I want it—right now." He isn't concerned about anyone else except insofar as someone else can do something for him. Of course, as he grows up, he realizes he must depend upon others and they don't always respond to his requests quickly. He finds he can influence their willingness to help him get what he wants by his attitude toward them, in either a positive or a negative way.

Of course, there are some people who seem always to operate on the premise of "what's in it for me." But most people grow beyond that total self-centered pattern. They really do feel good doing things for others, experiencing the truth of the Nigerian proverb: "When the right hand washes the left hand, the right hand becomes clean also."

A thank you can influence the attitude of others. Part of its importance is that a thank you tells someone they have filled a need in our life, and thus they have meaning, at least to us. We all seek to have meaning in life, to have a purpose. The purpose may be large and it may be small. Very few people make such great achievements that they win a Nobel prize. But everyone can make a difference in the life of at least one other person.

The wish to have a purpose was reflected in a Walt Disney television production, *Big Red*. An orphaned adolescent boy is talking with a wealthy middle-aged widower who has given him a job. "Mr. Boss" asks the youngster if he doesn't want to go to school to be able to make a lot of money. No, replies the youngster, "I want to go to school to find a purpose in life."

How nice it is when someone has a good day and "passes it on" to you. And people are so much more willing to do so when you show your appreciation. In the language of communications, it is "feedback." It is a message telling someone that they're doing a good thing, and keep it up. Indeed, if you don't get that feedback, you may not continue what you're doing.

An aunt used to get very upset when she gave us gifts for Christmas or a birthday and she didn't get a thank you note. The next time she would see the offending nephew or niece, she would ask if perhaps you really didn't want a gift? You had to be pretty dense not to get the message.

Therefore, "Thank you" can be vitally important. It is a "positive reinforcer," to use the vernacular of some behavioral scientists. And it does encourage us to do more things to earn those words.

Which prompts me to say to you, the reader, "Thank you." Thanks for the time you take to consider these thoughts. Thanks for the time many of you have taken to share your ideas with me. Thank you very much. And pass it on!